WINNING STRATEGIES IN SELLING

WINNING STRATEGIES IN SELLING

Jack Kinder, Jr.
Garry D. Kinder
Roger Staubach

Prentice-Hall, Inc. Englewood Cliffs, N.J.

Prentice-Hall International, Inc., *London*
Prentice-Hall of Australia, Pty. Ltd., *Sydney*
Prentice-Hall of Canada, Ltd., *Toronto*
Prentice-Hall of India Private Ltd., *New Delhi*
Prentice-Hall of Japan, Inc., *Tokyo*
Prentice-Hall of Southeast Asia, Pte., Ltd., *Singapore*
Whitehall Books, Ltd., *Wellington, New Zealand*

© 1981, *by*

PRENTICE-HALL, INC.

Englewood Cliffs, N.J.

Library of Congress Cataloging in Publication Data

Kinder, Jack
  Winning strategies in selling.

  Includes index.
  1. Selling. I. Kinder, Garry D.
II. Staubach, Roger. III. Title.
HF5438.25.K56   658.8′5   81-10518
ISBN 0-13-961128-2   AACR2

Printed in the United States of America

DEDICATION

Winners make things happen.

Losers let things happen.

This book was written for you and the count-less thousands who are committed to being self-motivated, independent winners in sell-ing.

THE BEST BOOK ON SELLING I HAVE EVER READ

FOREWORD BY EARL NIGHTINGALE

I was spending the summer in Carmel, California, when the call came through from Dallas, Texas. At first I thought the secretary was kidding. "Mr. Nightingale? Mr. Roger Staubach calling."

I had been a fan of Mr. Roger Staubach's since the time I saw him quarterbacking the Navy team in a game against Army. He was great then, and he's been great ever since. As you would imagine, he was friendly and easy to talk to. And when he mentioned the Kinder brothers, I remembered. On one of our many get-togethers, the Kinders had mentioned their friendship with Roger Staubach and what a super salesman and businessman he was.

I had known Jack and Garry Kinder since the old days in Chicago, back in the late 50's when they were executives with Equitable, the giant insurance company. Over the years I had come to know them as the best trainers of insurance people throughout all of North America. And that also applies to salesmen and women of all products and services, not just insurance by any means.

I had appeared on the platform with them at sales meetings and rallies many times and the better I got to know them, the more I liked, admired and respected them. They are men of the very highest moral calibre, both devout churchmen who have approached and taught their profession with the care, intelligence and integrity befitting any of the higher professions. To Jack and Garry Kinder, selling is an honorable, lifetime profession in which the rewards are as high as we want to set them and in which the whole man or woman and his or her family are taken into full consideration.

After reading this book, you will realize, as I did, that if you never read another on the selling profession, it will be quite sufficient.

What I had not known about Roger Staubach was that he earned more money selling, during the first three years he was with the Dallas Cowboys, than they were paying him. And that he had remained in sales right up to the present and had every intention of making it his life career.

As we chatted on the telephone we agreed that the quarter-back of a winning NFL team certainly had to be the best kind of salesman. His very demeanor, his attitude, the tone of his voice as he called the plays in the huddle and at the line of scrimmage, would determine, to a great extent, the spirit and attitude of the entire team. Roger mentioned that that was true and that working with the pass receivers was particularly important.

We're all selling, every day of our lives, whether we realize it or not. We're selling ourselves, most of all, and our habitual attitude tells the world how well or poorly we're succeeding. It shows in our eyes, the expressions on our faces, the way we walk, our posture, the way in which we enter a room and meet people. Our very *self-image* is a matter of salesmanship, as are the attitudes of our children and our spouses much of the time. We set the standard in our families, and that's selling. And our success, regardless of our line of work, will depend upon our selling skills.

Read this book, by all means. Don't read it in a hurry. Read it all. What you already know will not suffer from reminding and reinforcing or from considering a new approach. But most importantly, what you will find here are systems and strategies that never fail if they are faithfully followed. It is, simply, the best book on selling I have ever read. You will find it an endless source of enjoyment and lifelong profit.

Earl Nightingale

AUTHORS' INTRODUCTION

WE BELIEVE

We believe your main mission in selling is to win. Winning doesn't mean getting ahead of others. Winning means getting ahead of yourself. Winning means breaking your own records. It means outstripping your yesterdays by out-selling yourself today.

• • • • • •

We believe it can actually be *easier* to win than to lose in selling. But to win, you must do something that the "average" salesperson doesn't even consider; you must teach yourself to *think correctly*. You must think correctly about yourself, your selling ability, your prospects or clients, and your future in sales.

• • • • • •

We believe that this book will help you clarify your thinking in sales. Our combined 60 years in selling have taught us many things. Perhaps the most important is that right thinking comes to the individual who is reminded often of the following success factors.

1. You must be self-motivated.
2. You must not only want success, you must *need* it.
3. You must set a series of realistically high goals and establish a timetable for meeting them.
4. You must act as if it is *impossible* for you not to be a consistently high achiever.
5. You must form the habit of doing things the right way the *first time!*

• • • • • •

We believe that this book will make a difference in your selling career. We believe you will discover the "idea count" to be exceptionally high. The concepts and strategies are proven. They *are* transferable. We believe that they'll produce dynamic results for you.

· · · · · ·

We believe that you'll want to read, study and digest the information developed on these pages until the thoughts and suggestions become a dominant part of your selling equipment.

· · · · · ·

We believe that the tested techniques offered in this book will increase your sales and bring you greater commissions. This book encapsulates successful methods that have been used by some of America's leading salespeople. Chapter 4, for example, reveals the telephone selling tip that Jay Lewis utilized to increase his earnings by $2,000 each month.

As every salesperson is painfully aware, objections are a fact of life. Chapter 7 probes the most common reasons for objections, and then goes on to reveal a six-step strategy for overcoming all objections. Chapter 8 deals with the must crucial element of selling and provides you with the five cardinal rules that will make it much more likely that you will close the sale.

· · · · · ·

We believe that this is a book that will prove valuable to you in both your professional and your personal life. We believe that this is a book you will want to refer to again and again.

· · · · · ·

We believe this is the sure way for you to become a winner in selling!

Jack Kinder, Jr.
Garry D. Kinder
Roger Staubach

CONTENTS

CHAPTER 1

THE POWER OF A MADE-UP MIND IN SELLING

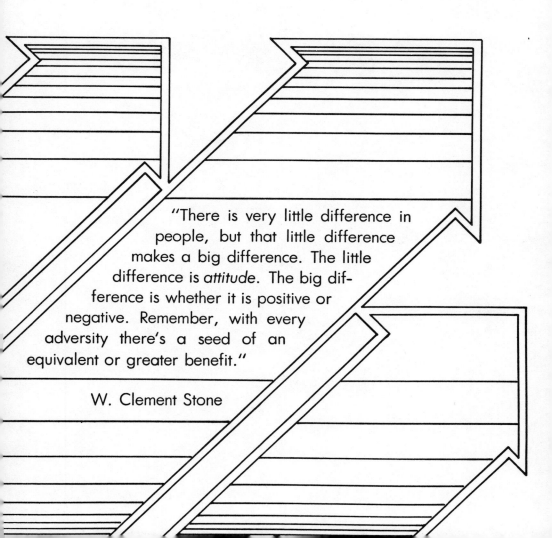

"There is very little difference in people, but that little difference makes a big difference. The little difference is *attitude*. The big difference is whether it is positive or negative. Remember, with every adversity there's a seed of an equivalent or greater benefit."

W. Clement Stone

MAKE UP YOUR MIND
THAT PREPARATION PAYS OFF

Metropolitan Stadium in Minneapolis is jam-packed. The NFL Eastern Championship is at stake. The Vikings have played the Cowboys tough. They are leading 14-10. Time is running out.

The Cowboys have moved the ball to midfield. The clock shows time left for one, maybe two, plays.

All-pro Drew Pearson goes deep. Drew and Viking defender Nate Wright are both streaking as hard as they can toward the end zone.

The ball is thrown high and long. A determined Drew Pearson, struggling for position and running at top speed, catches the ball on his hip. Drew holds on. The official signals touchdown. The Cowboys move up in front. The clock shows only 24 seconds left and the Cowboys go on to win 17-14!

Vikings fans thought Drew had interfered with Wright. The only thing known for certain in the stormy aftermath of the Cowboys' title victory was that Drew Pearson had scored the winning points. *Drew had a made-up mind about that catch!*

Spectacular achievements, like Drew's, are always preceded by unspectacular preparation.

The prepared professional captures the winning feeling. Professionals, in any human endeavor, because of preparation, act as if it were impossible to fail.

The scene changes—this time it's Texas Stadium. For nine consecutive times, the Philadelphia Eagles have met defeat at the hands of the Cowboys.

It became apparent, however, that the Eagles were "up" for this one. They established a third quarter lead that the Cowboys couldn't overcome and won the game 31-21.

Along with countless Cowboy fans, that's one game we'd like to forget. However, in the post-game remarks, Eagle Coach Dick Vermeil made a statement that we shouldn't forget: *"Our important victory tonight didn't just happen. This one we played without the fear of losing."* He went on to add, *"It started in the off-season and in training camp. It continued through a lot of tough days and nights. You can't believe the number of hours and the hard work that went into this winning performance!"*

Spectacular achievements are always preceded by unspectacular preparation.

success decision.

In professional football, it's called "paying the price." In the business world, it's called "self-discipline." In either case, it boils down to *deciding to succeed.* In fact, *not* to decide is *to* decide. If you haven't decided to succeed, you've decided to accept failure.

How do you decide to succeed? First of all, you ask yourself what you want out of your sales career. Once you decide, you plant that seed in your mind. Feed and nourish it as you would any valuable seed. Care for it. Imagine that seed sprouted and grown to maturity. Imagine yourself already harvesting that seed—already having achieved success! Picture yourself doing the things you will be doing when you've achieved your career goals!

Make up your mind that you must live off the fruit of your thoughts. What you think today or tomorrow, next month or next year, will mold your life and determine your future. Dr. Dennis Waitley, a national authority on high-level performance, says, "Be relentless in rehearsing your goal achievements. *Winning is a learned habit.*"

To paraphrase Shakespeare, "All things are ready if our minds are!" That's why it's so vitally important for you to make up your mind to act as though it were impossible to fail.

MAKE UP YOUR MIND ABOUT THE OPPORTUNITY

If you look at your work as a career instead of "just a job," the rewards of selling are substantial. A career in sales has one of the highest profit and satisfaction potentials of any field of endeavor—*if* you have self-discipline, courage and commitment.

The last census of the Department of Commerce showed that there are more people earning above $50,000 a year in sales than in any other profession—and many salespeople earn *twice* that amount or more!

What is the future for salespeople? First, we're on the threshold of the most exciting period of sales growth in history! Marketing, advertising and promotion have worked to make us not only aware of the benefits of technological advances but also of the rewards of financial planning and home comforts. *As never before, prospects are pre-conditioned to want the latest and the best.*

Secondly, the consumer is more affluent. Where once the bulk of our spendable income went for neccessities such as food, clothing, shelter and medical care, more and more consumer dollars are now available to be spent on other items. At the same time, companies and corporations are more willing than ever to look at new or more cost-efficient solutions to traditional problems.

It all adds up to an era of unprecedented opportunity. Make up your mind to be prepared to take full advantage of the opportunities the future will bring!

MAKE UP YOUR MIND ABOUT THE IMPORTANCE OF SALESMANSHIP

Unless you're a modern Robinson Crusoe and this book floated up on your beach in a bottle, you are engaged in sales. You use many of the principles of salesmanship in your daily contact with others. From cradle to grave, we are all salespeople.

To young people faced with the problems of earning a living or of merely getting along well with their associates, no other abilities will be more helpful than those practiced by effective salespeople. *Knowledge of selling principles is a vital element for successful living.*

Can selling be taught? We feel that the answer is

"yes!" Countless companies have either trained their own salespeople or have hired consultants to do the job. By their success, they've demonstrated over and over again that the principles of selling *can* be taught and learned just as surely as can the principles of engineering, law, medicine or athletics. Of course, you can't expect to become a skilled professional in any field without both study and practical experience. It's true that much *can* be learned by "trial and error"—but it's not an efficient use of time—and time in any profession is money.

Modern psychologists tell us that you are molded more by your environment than by your heredity. They insist that it is possible not only to modify your behavior, but even to alter your personality through training. Some go so far as to assert that environment and training can materially raise your I.Q. *Nearly everything essential to your success in selling can be acquired and developed.*

You will hear it said that "salespeople are *born* and not *made.*" While some people do seem to have a "natural" feel for selling, this statement is no more true of salespeople than it is of actors or artists or athletes. In fact, it's *easier* to "make" a salesperson than any other professional—as evidenced by the fact that there are more wealthy salespeople than wealthy quarterbacks!

An individual of only average talents can become an effective salesperson if he or she puts forth the required effort *consistently*. This same person might have no chance of ever becoming a great actor, famous artist or star quarterback for the Dallas Cowboys, *regardless* of effort!

Selling, at its best, is the art of creating in the mind of the prospect the idea that possession of your product or service best satisfies his or her need.

SALES DEFINED

Selling is the art of influencing prospects to buy at a mutual profit that which you are selling.

Selling is the art of understanding human desires and pointing the way to their fulfillment.

Selling is the art of assisting your prospects in buying intelligently. Your aim is not to make each transaction a "win or lose" situation but a "win-win" situation, because selling is the fine art of presenting your product or service in such a way that both seller and buyer feel they've gained something of value.

We've been saying that selling is an art, and it is. However, it is also a science. Science is a systematic knowledge, and art is knowledge made effective by skill.

When you systematically acquire selling knowledge, you're following a scientific approach. When you begin applying these scientific principles to your own products and services, you're practicing art.

There's a growing body of knowledge dealing with selling strategies. Your company provides you with a wealth of updated information about your products and services. Your industry and professional associations provide you with the opportunity to stay current and build your reservoir of knowledge. Selling is part science—because it takes applied research to be successful. It is also an art—because of the unique way that you apply your scientific knowledge to get the desired result.

Art can be poor, fair, good, excellent, or even a masterpiece; it all depends on how much skill the artist has and how he or she applies that skill.

Artists, we mentioned earlier, aren't born, they're made—just like salespeople. If you study the scientific part of selling and practice the art, you will produce good art and good results. You *will* be successful. No one else in the entire world can bring your unique experiences, your unique talent, your unique personality and your unique knowledge to your particular selling situation. With all of that going for you, you will be *successful—if* you have a burning desire for success!

MAKE UP YOUR MIND ABOUT PLAYING THE ODDS

After analyzing the work records of many, many salespeople, we have concluded that the typical salesperson produces little in the way of measurable results in five out of every six working hours! You don't sell to everybody you see, and much of what you do probably won't pay off for some time to come. So you see, very little time is actually spent *selling*.

If you look at your time from this standpoint, it could become discouraging. Furthermore, four out of every five people you call on will have a built-in sales resistance mechanism that can be very ego deflating. When you consider that over 80 percent of your sales time isn't spent selling and that 80 percent of your calls are apt to be negative, you might conclude that you can't beat the odds. But you can, if *you play the odds, and don't let the odds play you!*

Learn to play the odds. A pitcher doesn't strike out every batter he faces. Roger didn't throw a touchdown pass every time he got the ball. Babe Ruth is remembered as the home run king because he hit 714 home runs—but the Babe also struck out 1,330 times! The secret of success is to take each pitch as it comes and do your level best to knock it out of the park. Sure, you'll miss some. You'll even miss more than you hit—but you'll soon be hitting enough to make you a superstar!

To be a winner, you must be an odds player. You must have the self-generated brand of determination that carries you through to victory even though you operate in a negative atmosphere much of the time. Selling in many respects is more demanding than competitive athletics. Many salespeople operate without a coach or a team to support them—they have to build their own egos, recover from their own defeats, manage their own schedules and cheer their own victories. Salesmanship is a one-on-one kind of challenge, and that's what makes selling one of the most rewarding professions in the world!

MAKE UP YOUR MIND TO EXPECT GREAT THINGS

Everything about you—your facial expression, your movements, your dress, your tone of voice, the grip of your hand, the way you walk—tells your prospects what you think of yourself. You cannot disguise the impression you make even if you try. You can guard a few of your actions, but almost everything about you shows your estimate of yourself. There is no common law by which you can achieve selling success without first expecting it. *Great selling results are produced by the perpetual expectation of attaining them.* Despite natural talents, expanded through training and education, selling achievements will never rise higher than the expectation. People can who think they can. People can't who think they can't. It's an inflexible, indisputable law of selling and of life.

As a professional, your self-confidence is the one

thing you can never afford to surrender. Count as your enemy the person who shakes your estimate of your selling ability. Nothing enhances your ability like faith in yourself. In the selling profession, faith can make a one-talent salesperson into a great producer; but without it, a ten-talent sales rep remains mediocre.

The pros in selling are self-reliant, positive, optimistic and assured. They electrically charge the atmosphere they work in. *They have an aura of command that helps them convince their prospects that they can deliver—and deliver well—whatever they say they'll deliver.*

Set your mind so resolutely, so definitely and with such determined expectations toward the sales results you desire, that nothing on earth can sway your purpose. You will then draw to yourself the literal fulfillment of the promise: "For unto everyone that hath shall be given, and he shall have abundance."

MAKE UP YOUR MIND TO GIVE THE IMPRESSION OF SUCCESS AND CONFIDENCE

Make certain you look as if you *are* successful and as if you're accustomed to influencing people and closing sales. When you do, you will have something going for you the minute you face your prospect. Your prospect's natural reaction will be: "This individual must have a good idea or service, and maybe I should listen." All it takes to acquire such professional presence is careful attention to a few simple details.

From every point of view, it pays to dress well. It builds belief. Always look and dress like someone prospects would go to for advice. The first things prospects observe are your facial expressions, your voice and your teeth. These are all they have to go on until they get your initial message. Also, you owe it to yourself to maintain proper body weight. Make it a habit to check your weight on the scales frequently. Watching your eating habits and exercising regularly can be a mental tonic, too.

Observe the salespeople you think are the most outstanding. Don't you agree that they look successful? In selling, Shakespeare's advice is especially true: "The apparel often proclaims the person."

MAKE UP YOUR MIND TO GUARD MORAL VALUES

Few salespeople in any field ever reach the top without a strong sense of morality. The occasional sales rep who does gain a position of prestige without an honest character will eventually be uncovered. There is wisdom in the old adage, "Truth is the daughter of Time."

You are either honest or you are not. You cannot be a "little bit dishonest." If you are going to be a professional salesperson, then honesty has to become a way of life.

A reputation for honesty often pays off in dramatic ways. Donald Douglas built an aircraft company on his reputation for honesty and integrity. At one time, Donald was competing against Boeing to sell Eastern Airlines its first big jets. Eddie Rickenbacker, who headed Eastern, is said to have told Douglas that his specifications for the DC-8 were close to those of the Boeing 707 except for the noise suppression. He then gave Douglas one last chance to out-promise Boeing on this feature.

After consulting with his engineers, Douglas reported back that he didn't feel he could make the promise. Mr. Rickenbacker is said to have replied, "I know you can't. I wanted to see if you were still honest! You've got yourself an order for one hundred and sixty-five million dollars! Now go back and see if you can silence those jets anyway!"

A strong and sincere sense of morality is a prerequisite for winning in selling.

Make up your mind

- *about what it takes*
- *to give an impression of success*
- *to expect great things*
- *to act as though it were impossible for you to fail*
- *honesty is not the **best** policy, it is the **only** policy*

MAKE UP YOUR MIND TO BE A SOUND FINANCIAL MANAGER

Learn to keep your financial house in order. Most people entering selling must be taught to be money managers. However, it has been our experience that the faculty for being a good financial manager is much like that of being a good golfer—it is not so much *taught* as it is *caught*.

A Louisville consultant, Ken Lutz, recommends to clients, "Form the habit early in your business life of living on 50 percent of your gross income. Sound money management dictates that you set aside 10 percent for church and charities."

Lutz goes on to say, "Next, pay yourself by saving 10 percent. Thirty percent of your gross income is to be earmarked for city, county, state, federal and social security taxes no matter what you do. Fifty percent is all that's left."

You've heard some say, "This sounds good, and the minute I get my bills caught up, I'm going to start the program." That won't get it done. Embrace the "Lutz Formula," learn to live on 50 percent of your gross income. You may not achieve this goal each year, but without a plan, you have no chance at all. Start this practice today and reap the benefits throughout your career. *The condition of your financial balance sheet is generally a reliable measurement of the balance you are achieving in your life.*

MAKE UP YOUR MIND YOU FEEL BETTER WHEN YOU FEEL FIT

Dr. O. Carl Simonton, M.D., is the director of the famed Cancer Counseling and Research Center in Fort Worth, Texas. Dr. Simonton has spent years teaching patients to use their minds to alter the course of their malignancies. In his best seller, *Getting Well Again,* Dr. Simonton writes about the power of a made-up mind. He says, "The results of our approach to cancer treatment made us confident of this conclusion—*a positive mental participation can influence the onset of disease, the outcome of treatment and quality of life.*"

Dr. Kenneth Cooper, author of the best-selling book, *Aerobics,* says he wishes more people would be as fresh at five o'clock in the afternoon as they were at seven in the morning. Dr. Cooper says, "I would like to see fewer hospitals and rest homes for curing illness and diseases and more conditioning centers for their prevention." The great scientist Thomas Edison predicted Cooper's approach when he said, "The doctor of the future will give no medicine, but will interest the patient in the care of the human frame, in diet and in the cause and prevention of disease."

Dr. Cooper offers the following advice for anyone who plans to embark upon an exercise program:

1. Have a complete physical and make certain that your doctor approves your program.

2. Regularity is the most important element of your program. Try to maintain a frequency of five workouts a week. Four is adequate, though not ideal; three is a bare minimum. Therefore, choose an activity that you will do regularly.

3. For running, obtain a good pair of running shoes. Each shoe is structurally different, so you may want to try a variety to find the best fit for you.

4. If you are just beginning a program of exercise, start slowly and comfortably. This helps prevent muscle and joint injuries. Also, do not hesitate to reduce your workouts should you sustain an injury or illness or for some other reason have an enforced layoff.

5. Adequate warm-up and cool-down is also important. Simple stretching exercises to loosen muscles and help prevent injuries are helpful prior to exercise. Never sit or lie down immediately after exercise or go directly to the whirlpool, steam room or shower. A slow cool-down for about five minutes

will allow for adequate readjustment of your cardiovascular system.

The aerobics point system is a method of quantifying the cardiopulmonary benefits of various types of exercise. Studies show that 25-30 points per week are necessary to achieve and maintain an acceptable level of fitness. Examples of a 30 points per week program are:

- Run two miles in less than 20 minutes four times a week.
- Swim 800 yards in less than 20 minutes four times a week.
- Walk three miles in less than 45 minutes five times a week.
- Cycle five miles in less than 20 minutes six times a week.

The significance of keeping physically fit was demonstrated in a fitness program conducted in cooperation with the U.S. Public Health Service. After one year in the program, participants were given physical examinations and filled out questionnaires concerning their health, attitudes and behavior. Eighty-nine percent thought that they had greater stamina. But, just as importantly, 60 percent indicated that they had a more positive attitude toward their jobs and that their work performance had improved—and *half* felt less strain and tension!

Why is physical fitness so important for salespeople? In preparing this book, we were privileged to study many top performers, and one characteristic stood out above all the others—this characteristic was *energy. Energy*—the ability to work hard and long—isn't possible unless your body is in top condition.

Lynn Hutchings is an example of what energy combined with dedication can mean to a professional in selling.

Lynn earns over $200,000 a year in selling in Rock Springs, Wyoming (population about 35,000)! To do it, Lynn started on the ground floor, working 15 to 16 hours a day, seven days a week.

"I loved it, and I can say I still do," Lynn told us. "Frankly, I love every minute of it. I try to take more time off now for the family, but I still work long and hard." Lynn has shattered every company record—in spite of the fact that he's in a small market.

Roger, of course, is a person with a high energy level. Roger's fitness has equipped him to perform not only on the field but in the office as well. Roger never really knew when an injury might end his football career, so right after his Navy discharge, he began preparing for a dual career—football and selling.

Roger went to the Henry S. Miller Company's new insurance division. He attended insurance schools because he wanted to sell the best product possible. Roger found an annuity policy that he really believed in. He studied that policy and every policy it competed with. It took a lot of hours, a lot of study and a lot of cold calls—a lot of energy. Yet Roger sold over $1,000,000 in only four months—including a substantial key-man policy to a Dallas executive.

Roger's accomplishments as a quarterback are well known. A lesser known fact is that, during his first three years with the Dallas Cowboys, he made more money *selling* than he did playing football!

That takes energy, both mental and physical!

MAKE UP YOUR MIND
THAT LEADERS ARE READERS

Newton D. Baker, nationally known attorney and member of President Woodrow Wilson's cabinet, said, "The person who graduates today and stops learning tomorrow is uneducated the day after." Feed your mind as you would feed your body—regularly and with a balanced diet.

There are two types of knowledge you should acquire from reading: *people* knowledge and *product* knowledge. To do this, you should read *at least* one book every month to improve your mind. Charlie "Tremendous" Jones once said, "Chances are you'll be about the same person in five years as you are today—except for the people you meet and the books you read." Charlie also points out that the person who *won't* read really isn't much better off than the person who *can't* read!

Keeping abreast of changes and staying well informed is far more important in sales today than ever before. It's also more difficult than it's ever been because changes occur so rapidly. Your prospects are both sophisticated and demanding. They expect you to have a working knowledge of many subjects. There is more to know and more to read—and more things competing for your time.

Power Reading is a self-instructional program developed by Bill Munn and Dr. Gene Davenport of the Kinder Institute in Dallas. It has a proven success record for improving both reading speed and reading retention. Since good reading skills are a must for today's salesperson, we suggest that you investigate *Power Reading* if you wish to improve your own reading skills.

What should you read? Trade journals and publications, of course. But, also form the habit of reading books that teach you to think, work, sell and live. Study books that will help you be more effective in dealing with yourself and others. Make it a habit to read the *Wall Street Journal, Business Week, Fortune, Nation's Business, Reader's Digest* and *Success Unlimited.* If you are a religious person, or if you want to learn about "the book of books," read and study the Bible. There's no end to its treasures.

As T. B. Smith wrote, "Books extend our narrow present back to the limitless past. They show us the mistakes of those before us and share with us the recipes for human success. There's nothing to be done that books will not help us to do better." That's the reason *sales leaders are readers.*

MAKE UP YOUR MIND TO KEEP YOUR FAMILY LIFE IN ORDER

Obviously, your family is the primary social institution in your life. Along the way, you're sure to discover the importance and the difficulty of scheduling time with them. When you're new in selling, you must spend a lot of time on the job. You have to arrange interviews at times when prospects will see you. This means you will be working many evenings and weekends, until you become established and have built a clientele. This makes it especially difficult to find "the right time" to spend with your family. That's why we urge you to schedule time for them.

It is not always the quantity of time spent with your

spouse and children, but the quality of time that will make the big difference. Plan, schedule and spend quality time with your family on a regular basis. Plan family vacations and outings. Sunday is a good day to devote to your family. It is a time when you can worship together or plan other activities as a family. It is the only day that everyone can be at home together. *You cannot separate your family responsibilities from your personal development.*

As Roger says, "Having your family life in order really helps your confidence in other areas of your life, too. If you find you just don't have *time* for your family and your business, then you're too busy. You need to either reschedule your business or redirect your career paths. When I sensed that I wasn't able to put in the quantity or quality of time I wanted to with my family, it helped to move up my decision to leave professional football."

Your family can be your biggest career booster. Unfortunately, we find that too many salespeople only tell their families the negative things about their business—never the positive. When Roger was quarterback for the Dallas Cowboys, he was always careful to never let doubt or disappointment show on his face—because he knew that discouragement is a contagious disease among football teams. Take care to spread positive thoughts and share successes with your family. Talk freely about your accomplishments and goals and demonstrate a positive attitude toward your selling job and its future.

You'll find that your family is your biggest booster, your cheering *section—if* you consider them in your decisions and invite them to be a part of your success team!

MAKE UP YOUR MIND
IT'S THE SPIRITUAL THAT
DETERMINES THE MATERIAL

The first and perhaps most important area for seeking personal excellence is in the realm of the spiritual. "Our greatest need is for a spiritual improvement in ourselves," says the well-known author Arthur Toynbee in his book *Surviving the Future*. Toynbee says, "There is an ultimate spiritual reality which gives the universe its meaning and value." H. G. Wells said it this way: "Until a person has found God, he or she begins at no beginning, he or she works to no end." The spiritual life is the base from which every other area of one's life evolves.

Your own spiritual life is quite a personal matter and we would not presume to tell you what you should or should not do. However, we do know you can't separate what you do from what you are. We became convinced at an early age that daily prayer and regular church attendance help immeasurably to keep one's spiritual life in balance.

When Roger was working for the Henry S. Miller Company, Henry S. Miller, Jr., had a sign on his desk that said simply, "INTEGRITY." Because he *lived* it, it meant something to every employee that he met. We need to keep a mental image of that "INTEGRITY" plaque before us at all times. If you have a spiritual undergirding, it is easier to live up to—because those of us with spiritual convictions have an absolute standard to live up to. If you don't, then there is always the temptation to make moral and ethical compromises—and time has a way of uncovering all shortcomings.

We never will forget the Watergate hearings when someone asked Jeb Stuart MacGruder, "How could an intelligent, outstanding young man like you get involved with this mess?" MacGruder thought a moment, hung his head and said, "I don't know. I guess I just lost my moral compass."

We're reminded of Robert Burns who, as he lay on his deathbed, turned to his nephew and, patting his well-worn Bible, said, "Read the book and be a good man and when you come to the place in your life where I am now, you'll know that's all that is important."

Make up your mind

- *to be a student*
- *to stay physically fit*
- *to be a sound financial manager*
- *to keep your family life in order*
- *to stay spiritually strong*

THE POWER OF THE MADE-UP MIND ILLUSTRATED

When Roger graduated from Annapolis, he had a four-year stint to serve with the United States Navy. Everyone doubted that he could come back after a tour in Vietnam and ever play pro ball—except for Roger and the Dallas Cowboys.

Yet Roger threw the football to anyone who would catch it while on duty. And while he was at his last duty station, in Pensacola, Florida, he was quarterback for the base football team, the Navy Goshawks.

When he was discharged, he went to the Cowboys and

got his first real chance in the fifth exhibition game—and led the team to victory. In the next game, against Baltimore, Roger ran 118 yards, threw four interceptions and Dallas lost 23-7. Bubba Smith, Baltimore's defensive end, said, "I never ran so much in my life chasing anybody. I don't ever want to play against that cat again."

Yet, Roger still had a made-up mind that he could not only make it in the pro league, but that he could become starting quarterback. Sometimes, the power of Roger's made-up mind wasn't transferable. The evening before the next game, against the St. Louis Cardinals, he told Coach Landry, "Do you realize just a year ago today I was the starting quarterback for the Pensacola Navy Goshawks against Middle Tennessee State in Murfreesboro, Tennessee? And just think, Coach, now I'm starting in the Cotton Bowl for the Dallas Cowboys against the St. Louis Cardinals!"

Roger remembers that Coach Landry just got a sick look on his face and walked away without replying.

The Cowboys defeated the Cardinals 24-3. After the game, Landry told Roger, "You'll do all right in this league. Don't worry about it."

Jack Kinder's favorite story about the power of a made-up mind concerns his close friend, Tommy John, who won 20 games pitching for the Los Angeles Dodgers in 1977. He went on to pitch the winning game in the National League playoffs and finished second in the voting for the coveted Cy Young award. The next season, he was signed as a free agent by the New York Yankees. In June of 1980, Tommy earned his 200th career victory against the Seattle Mariners—a victory that caused Seattle Manager Darrell Johnson to say, "The man was outstanding, that's for sure. John knows what he's doing. He's a master craftsman."

This record alone is enough to earn Tommy John a permanent place in the record books—but there's more. Back in 1974, Tommy approached the All-Star break with the best record in the National League. While pitching against the Montreal Expos, he felt a sudden tearing sensation in his arm, as though his arm had been ripped from its socket and was flying off at right angles to his body.

In surgery, it was revealed that his ligament was completely torn and unrecognizable, that the muscles that arose from the inner side of his arm above the elbow were torn loose and had slipped two inches toward the wrist. The doctors transplanted a tendon, saying that there was only 1 chance in 100 that he would ever pitch again.

Tommy did pitch again, but lost feeling in his fingers. Another operation seemed to help, but Tommy's pitching stubbornly refused to come back—two fingers were paralyzed.

One day, Tommy overheard a teammate say, "What's he trying to prove? He's finished. Why doesn't he face up to it?"

In church one Sunday, Tommy prayed for a miracle—and began working as if the miracle was on its way. Slowly, painfully, with no doubt that he would not only play baseball, but play winning baseball, Tommy worked and exercised and asked to be shifted to the Instructional League. Again, Tommy John struck out batters. He had climbed another rung back on the ladder to success—the ladder that's grounded on a made-up mind!

Roger Staubach's favorite story about the power of the made-up mind concerns a high school nose guard who was born with one leg. The youth's name is Carl Joseph and he attended Madison High School in

Madison, Florida. Although Carl was born with one leg and doesn't even have a thigh on the left side, he never thought of himself as handicapped. In Madison's 5-5 season of 1979, Carl played both offense and defense, blocked two punts and deflected two passes. He also fought his way through blockers to down the opposing quarterback in varsity competition.

Carl only has one leg, but he's worked and built that leg into a tree trunk. His upper body is so strong that he can keep blockers away from him—and he can literally *hop* so fast that he was not only a threat on the football field, but in basketball and track! He was a high jumper on the track team and threw discus and shot. He won dual meets with high jumps of 5′10″.

Carl's power of the made-up mind enabled him to do the "seemingly impossible." Yet, he *does* have a handicap—in spite of the fact that the state of Florida removed him from the welfare rolls. "Anyone who can play football can't be handicapped," they said. Madison Coach Frank Yannossy says, "He never used his handicap as an excuse. He did everything in practice. He took part in every drill. He just threw his crutches aside and went at it."

Yannossy doesn't like to exaggerate. "I don't think Carl will play in college," he says. "It would just be too tough. But, he's been an inspiration to our teams and our schools. He's very religious; he gave the blessing at our pre-game meals. He's the type of kid I wish my own son would grow up to be like."

Another story that illustrates the power of the made-up mind that we all like is the story of Raul Jimenez, owner of Jimenez Food Products, Inc., who has grown from being a migrant worker to a millionaire.

Raul began in a 17′ × 14′ room making Mexican

sausage, tamales and hot sauce back in 1953. Today, his company grosses about $14 million a year and his operation spans most of Texas. His *customers* span the globe.

When Raul began, they mixed everything by hand—because they couldn't *afford* electric mixers. He had never had a bank account and, when asked by a supplier for a "financial statement," he had to turn to a friend to find out what the man was talking about!

What makes Raul's story even more exciting is the fact that he began his business at age 21—and only had a *seventh-grade education!*

In a recent article in *Southwest Airlines Magazine,* Raul was quoted as saying, "I learned a lot of things the hard way. You have to have drive and a goal. Anyone can make it, if you're determined and persistent, with a faith in God. That's my formula for being successful."

Never be a quitter. Quitters never win, and winners never quit!

Excellent advice! It's another way of saying what W. W. Clements, Chairman of the Board of the Dr Pepper Company, is fond of saying. "Foots," as Mr. Clements' friends call him, began has career with the Dr Pepper Company as a route salesman, driving a delivery truck in Tuscaloosa, Alabama, in 1935. It was under his leadership that Dr Pepper became a national soft drink in 1970 after 85 years as a regional beverage. Today, it ranks in the top four soft drinks in America. "Foots" says, "Success is never final—and neither is failure—unless *you* let it be!"

Quitters never win and winners never quit. Or, if you

prefer, success is never final and neither is failure—unless you let it be.

This brings us to Garry Kinder's favorite power of the made-up mind story. It's a negative kind of story that points out the antithesis of a made-up mind.

The boxer with the quickest hands and the fastest feet became the world's heavyweight champion. Many have called him the greatest boxer of all times.

In our opinion, he became that kind of performer not because of his quick hands and fast feet, but because of his positive mental attitude. Muhammad Ali was so positive in his approach that he would even predict the round in which his opponent would fall. Interestingly enough, his opponents seemed to cooperate willingly. This continued for many years, until his featured match with an able contender, Joe Frazier. Sports writers asked Ali, "What is your feeling about this important championship fight?" Ali responded, "If Joe Frazier wins, a lot of people will be glad. If I win, a lot of people will be sad." Notice the word *"if"*—it was the first time ever that there was a crack in Ali's positive-approach armor. As you will remember, Frazier captured the heavyweight crown by upsetting the unbeatable champion. This is another example of the power of the made-up mind—or lack of it!

Perhaps the greatest of all stories on the will to succeed—the power of the made-up mind—centers on Pete Strudwick. Pete, a 50-year-old Californian, had an ambition to be a marathon runner. A marathon is 26 miles, 385 yards. This determined competitor has run and completed more than 40 marathons, including the Boston Marathon—*and he has no feet.* No feet! Pete runs on stumps.

Someone asked him, "Pete, how do you run 26 miles

with no feet?" He replied, "You don't lean backwards!"

In order for *you* to realize your full potential in selling, you must develop the kind of persistence that comes only from a made-up mind. A favorite quotation of ours is this one by Calvin Coolidge: "Nothing in the world can take the place of persistence. Talent will not; nothing is more common than unsuccessful people with talent. Genius will not; unrewarded genius is almost a proverb. Education alone will not; the world is full of educated derelicts. Persistence and determination alone are omnipotent."

We often hear it said of a salesperson: "Everything he or she touches turns to gold." We sometimes think of these high achievers as being lucky. The fact is, their selling success is the result of a made-up mind—their willpower. By the force of their convictions they wring success from the most adverse circumstances.

Coach Tom Landry wrote a great statement entitled *Willpower:*

"Intellect tires, the will never,
The brain needs sleep, the will none,
The whole body is nothing but objectified will,
The whole nervous system contributes the
    antennae of the will,
Every action of the body is nothing but the act of
    the will objectified."

THE POWER OF THE
MADE-UP MIND SUMMED UP

Your power to persuade others originates from your philosophies and beliefs. Your selling philosophies determine the attitudes you develop and the habits you form. The principles of selling and living that you adhere to will move you up to join the salespeople who get to the top and stay there. *Make up your mind* to live by these principles.

Make up your mind that you are your most important customer. You must be sold on your job, your products and your ability to perform.

Make up your mind that your product or service, properly sold, is of considerably more value to your buyer than any commission you can possibly earn.

Make up your mind that time is money and that learning to manage your time productively will be one of your most profitable achievements.

Make up your mind to believe in the law of averages and the wisdom of knowing the dollar value of each of your primary activities.

Make up your mind that honest, intelligent effort is always rewarded.

Make up your mind that a selling interview is *never* to be considered a contest between you and your prospect. It is always to be a "win-win" encounter.

Make up your mind that the power of your sales presentation will always lie in its simplicity.

Make up your mind that the purchase must be "helped along" and is most often made because you guide the prospect's behavior in an effective, organized manner.

Make up your mind that people buy today, not nearly as much because they understand your product thoroughly, but because they feel and believe that you understand them, their problems and the things they want to accomplish.

Make up your mind that almost all development is, in

fact, self-development—that personal growth is the product of practice, observation and self-correction.

Make up your mind that vigorous physical conditioning is a prerequisite for maintaining a high level of energy.

Make up your mind that sales leaders are ordinary people with the extraordinary determination to make every occasion a great occasion.

Make up your mind to believe in the truth; that it is the spiritual that always determines the material.

Make up your mind that there is great power in holding a high ideal of the products and services you are selling. The model your mind holds, your lifestyle is certain to copy.

These are the kinds of philosophies you find held by those salespeople who have warranted pride in their accomplishments. Study them. Digest them. Make them a dominant part of your selling strategy and you will find yourself among those pros in selling who not only "make it to the top," but *stay* at the top.

THE POWER OF THE MADE-UP MIND REMINDERS

- Spectacular achievements in selling are always preceded by unspectacular preparation.
- Selling is the art of assisting your prospects to buy intelligently.
- In selling, the result is always your final judge.
- Selling achievements never rise higher than the expectations.
- The condition of your financial balance sheet is

generally a reliable measurement of the balance you are achieving in your life.

- Readers become leaders.
- Personal growth is the product of observation, self-correction and practice.
- Sales leaders are ordinary people with an extraordinary determination to make every occasion a great one.
- It's the spiritual that always determines the material.

CHAPTER 2

PLANNING AND PROSPECTING: THE CORNERSTONES OF WINNING SELLING

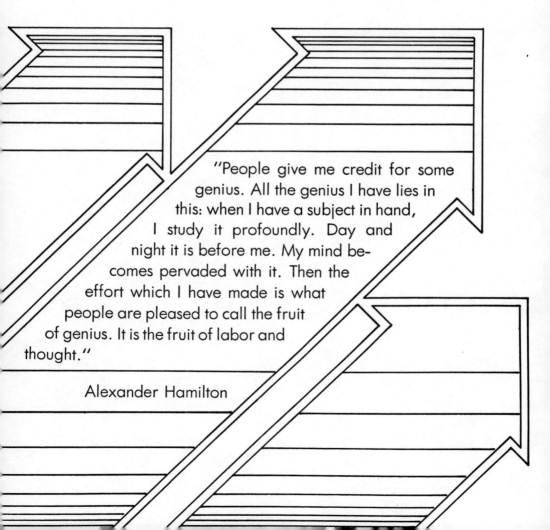

"People give me credit for some genius. All the genius I have lies in this: when I have a subject in hand, I study it profoundly. Day and night it is before me. My mind becomes pervaded with it. Then the effort which I have made is what people are pleased to call the fruit of genius. It is the fruit of labor and thought."

Alexander Hamilton

EXAMINING THE SELLING
SPECTRUM

Regardless of the "position they play," professionals have a strong belief in the basics. In selling, the professional keeps returning to the basics of planning and prospecting until they become knit with habit.

Before looking at these basics, let's examine an array of positions which comprise the selling spectrum. Think particularly of your job and of the creative skill required in each of the following:

"Suppliers." This salesperson's job is to deliver the product, such as fuel oil, milk, bread, soft drinks. Selling responsibilities are secondary. Efficient service and a pleasant manner will enhance customer satisfaction, leading to more sales. Not many sales are originated by suppliers.

"Interceptors." This salesperson's job is pretty much being an "order taker." Examples are the clothing sales clerk or a furniture store clerk. Here, the prospects have already made up their minds to buy. The salesperson's job is to serve the customer. The salesperson's aim may be to use suggestive selling and upgrade the merchandise purchased. Opportunities to do more than that are limited. Also, interceptors sometimes work in the field as order takers, such as for soap, beverages, perfumes.

"Educators." This salesperson is called upon to educate or to build goodwill with the potential user. Examples are the medical detailer representing a pharmaceutical house or a university representative.

"Generators." These are positions that demand the creative sale of tangible products, such as automobiles, real estate and encyclopedias, and intangibles such as life insurance, advertising, stocks and bonds. Generators must make the prospect dissatisfied with his or her present situation, then begin to sell their product. Intangible products are generally more difficult for the prospect to comprehend. Intangibles are less readily demonstrated and dramatized.

Each type of sales position requires its own unique configuration of traits, attributes and qualities. *However, the basic habits of planning and prospecting are prerequisites to success in each of the described positions.*

THE WAY IN IS EASY—
THE WAY OUT IS HARD

Psychologists tell us that we are governed by habit. They say every salesperson develops habits of thought and action that are good or bad, effective, regular or spasmodic. Dryden said, "We first make our habits, and then our habits make us." This is especially true in regard to your sales career. *Your habits determine your behavior and your style.* It's obvious that you can attain real success only if you consciously develop habits that are sound, effective and regular.

One time we came across a truly great thought on

habit building. It went like this: "The way in is easy—the way out is hard." Think about that one. Haven't you found the "way in" to poor dieting, exercising and living habits to be easy, *really* easy? But, haven't you found that the "way out" of those habits is extremely hard?

If you are a follower of competitive Olympic swimming matches, you know that most of the title holders are comparatively young—young men and women considerably under twenty. You know also that almost invariably these title holders are registered in the name of an athletic club, which means that from childhood they have been swimming under supervision. From their first day in the pool, breathing, stroke, rhythm and coordination have been carefully coached and checked.

These young athletes become gold medal winners before they are old enough to vote because they learn good habits from the beginning. They never have to take time out to *unlearn* bad habits and to replace them with good habits. They discover at the very start the "way in" to good habits is easy—the "way out" is hard.

It is the same with the planning and prospecting habits that you build. The "way in" to sound habits will be easy if you follow the procedures developed in this chapter.

THE PLANNING FUNCTION

Planning is just as important as doing, and adequate planning should always take place before doing.

Many salespeople confuse *activity* with *accomplishment*. As far as effort is concerned, an individual running around in circles can be working as hard as the person running down the street, but certainly not getting as far. To maximize your results, you should recognize that planning and doing must work together, with planning always preceding doing.

Planning is the base upon which all future action should take place. Planning awakens you to opportunities and shows you the way to their realization—it is the link between desire and realization.

Planning is ongoing; it is a never-ending activity. In Chapter 12 we will examine in-depth the annual planning process we recommend. But, for now, let's look at planning your day, your week and your month.

PLAN TO WAKE UP EMPLOYED

Form the habit of planning each day's calls and activities the previous day. Plan at the same hour and at the same place. You will be amazed at the creative thoughts that will begin to flow to you during this "planning hour."

Henry Doherty, the great industrialist, said, "I can hire people to do everything but two things: *think* and *do things in the order of their importance.*"

On Normandy Boulevard in Jacksonville, Jim Tatum gets his thinking and priorities right each day. Jim Tatum has earned the reputation for selling more men's suits each year than any other clothing salesman in the United States. "It's the 90-minute planning habit I established 20 years ago that has made it all possible. I have the Holy Bible in front of me and legal pad for planning the priorities. It's my most important discipline. The dividends it has paid me are enormous."

The daily plan habit assures you of waking up each day employed. First, you decide what is to be done. Then, you decide upon priorities. This daily discipline boils down to the trite but effective principle, "Plan your work and work your plan."

SUBSCRIBE TO THE "BOX TIME" THEORY

The "Box Time" theory is an approach used by successful salespeople to focus on the priority jobs. Purchase a daily planning calendar, one with a box or space for each hour of your work week. Plan your time so that you're always either in front of a prospect or endeavoring to be there.

The "Box Time" discipline keeps you focused. It reduces the times when other people or things can disturb your momentum or crowd your day with nonproductive activities.

PLAN A MONTHLY SELF-ORGANIZATION DAY

It's always easy to throw a number of prospect cards together as you start the month and think you are prepared. That doesn't take much time.

However, to plan the upcoming month carefully, to prepare proposals, write letters, schedule calls in their proper order, requires an intensified effort. We recommend setting aside a half day at each month's end and thinking of it as "Self-Organization Day." You'll find it pays you big dividends.

Two key planning benefits:

1. *desired results are defined and*
2. *deadlines are clearly estab-*
   lished

THE BEST KEPT SALES SECRET

The best kept sales secret is this: *Do the most important things first.* And, in selling, the most important things are the few factors that make the big difference in obtaining results. When you learn to focus your time, thinking and energy on these, your success is virtually assured.

Tom Tierney is a master salesman—one of the best we have ever known. Here is one of the reasons. Tom says, "I remind myself often that I'm paid for the *results* I produce and not the *work* I do." Tom has formed the habit of recognizing priorities and staying focused on them.

Of course, interruptions will come—learn to anticipate them. Plan a certain time each day to deal with interruptions like phone calls and return them all at that time. You'll only get frustrated trying to "work your plan" if you don't allow for interruptions.

One of the great satisfactions in life comes from being productive, getting things done. If you are having trouble getting organized and being at your best, remember there is only one way: Take more time to think and to do things in the order of their importance. *The secret to improved effectiveness generally lies not in working more hours, but in making the hours work more for you.* You do this with proper planning of your sales time.

THE PROSPECTING FUNCTION

Prospecting successfully on a consistent basis boils down to two things: paying attention and using memory "ticklers" to bring things to mind when you need them. Both are necessary to be successful in any type of sales—but if you're in a business where you must generate all or part of your own prospects, they're absolutely vital!

Let's look at "paying attention" first.

Paying Attention

"You see," Sherlock Holmes admonished Dr. Watson, "but you do *not* observe!" Opportunities come our way each day. We "see" them, but we do not "observe." To put it another way, we see opportunities, but we don't examine them closely enough to get any real value from them.

Successful salespeople *observe.* They keep their eyes and ears open. They make notes. They develop an alertness and a probing, inquisitive attitude.

When Roger was quarterback for the Dallas Cowboys, they studied game films of the team they were to play days in advance. They didn't just "see" the film, like a person would say, "Yeah, I *saw* the game!"—they *observed!* They took notes. They watched key plays over and over until they knew how the other team acted and reacted and, as nearly as possible, they knew how they *thought.*

When Roger was off the field and in his real estate office, he applied the same powers of observation to prospects. He learned what kind of properties each investor was interested in—what his or her buying motives were. He learned to try and think like the prospect would think—and built a successful business!

Paying attention can become one of the greatest factors in your sales success story! You don't just see with your optic nerves, you see with your mind. Paying attention is a powerful mental process. It keeps your mind on the material that your eye brings it, considering, forming opinions, planning, estimating, evaluating, weighing, balancing and calculating.

Paying attention is a key to increasing your production. It prompts you to learn as much as possible about the prospects you're calling on—their reputation and capacity, from whom they are buying now, and what value they are getting from their dollar.

Paying attention helps you do your homework and plan each call in advance. It makes it possible for you to evaluate prospects' problems carefully and to decide upon the best ways to help them solve their problems.

Mona Biscamp pays attention. Mona has sold over $100 million in residential sales in the nine years she has represented the Henry S. Miller Company. *"You prospect 24 hours a day,"* Mona advises. "I make it a practice to ask everyone I come in contact with two questions. Are you thinking about listing your home or buying a new one? Then, who do you know who is?"

"Alertness is the key to the success I've enjoyed," Mona adds. Learn to pay attention—it will pay you substantial dividends throughout your career—*if* you organize the data so that it's available to you whenever you're ready to use it. That brings us to "ticklers."

The "Tickler" System

A "Tickler" system is merely a formal program for bringing bits of data to your mind and to help you locate information you need. A prospecting "tickler" begins with a simple 3 × 5 file box with tab cards—the kind available at any office supply or stationery store.

Into this file you'll place the names of clients and prospects and any other important follow-up information. The primary purpose of the file is to provide you with a system for bringing the names of prospects to your attention at the time when it's most logical to see them. Your "tickler" box should be divided into two sections: an alphabetical section and a "when-to-see" section that you'll arrange by months.

Make every effort you can in every call to get enough information to enable you to know the best time and the strongest reason for seeing your prospect at a future date. Enter the important information on your prospect card and file it in the proper month. Obviously, you want a build-up of qualified prospects in your "when-to-see" reservoir. Effective field work produces a constant movement of prospect calls from the alphabetical section to the "when-to-see" reservoir.

Don't develop a hope chest. It's not a sign of success to have a bulging box of ticklers if your box is full of dead wood. Determine as early as possible whether the person is a prospect for you and whether or not you can make a sale with a reasonable amount of follow-up. If you can't, then eliminate the card from your system. *The only tickler system that works is one that contains bona fide prospects—the kind you can see and sell!*

A large file box made up of dead wood is an impediment. It gets in your way. It fools you into believing you're doing a good job of prospecting when all you're doing is a good job of filing. A box of dead wood invites you to spend idle hours sorting and resorting cards. It's better to have a tickler box with a hundred "prospects" than one with a thousand "suspects."

The good prospector with a well-organized, active tickler system must work hard to find enough time to see all of the prospects he or she has.

We live and sell in a generation of hustle-bustle. "Time out" for thinking and organization is sometimes considered idling your motor when you should be racing out to meet someone. At one time, prospecting may have been thought of as taking time out from selling, but for today's successful sales professionals prospecting is number one on their list of priorities.

All of us keep our tickler file boxes right on our desks where we can get at them. Roger has formed the habit of carrying a notebook in his pocket at all times. Whenever he gets information he can use, he jots it down and then transfers it later to his tickler box. "It's so easy to forget things," Roger says. "It may be a name, it may be data on a deal that might work out for me. It might even be information that won't be ripe to use for two years—in that case, I transfer it to a central file."

You'll also want to add names to your tickler box that didn't work out the first time you tried them but might later. Maybe a prospect got up on the wrong side of the bed the day you called, but you know that you have something he or she needs. You put that person in the tickler file and try again later.

Roger says, "I've run into people who just had a dominant type of personality and, maybe the first time you met, you just approached them wrong. If later you decide that your approach should be to fight dominance with dominance, then you make a note of that. Three months later, you can come back to the same client and you know how to deal with him or her— you've got the product or service he or she wants and now you know how to present your case—and you've made a sale!"

> *"All good selling starts with a prospective buyer who can make a decision."*

EXAMINE THESE SIX PROSPECTING STRATEGIES

Someone has suggested that prospecting is the search "for needers who can be changed first into wanters and then into buyers." *To get more buyers you must discover more prospects.* The vital importance of getting names of people who might be needers is so well recognized that six key strategies have been worked out to assist you in becoming more effective as a prospector.

We've made no effort to list these in order of importance because, quite frankly, none of us *exactly* agree on the ranking. Their relative importance will vary with individuals and, of course, with professions, but all six are vital and none of the six can be neglected.

They are:

- the personal observation strategy
- the endless chain strategy
- the center-of-influence strategy

- the junior associate strategy
- the direct mail strategy
- the cold canvass strategy

Let's examine them in more detail.

1. The personal observation strategy. This consists of being constantly on the alert for prospect leads no matter where you are or with whom you are. Prospects are everywhere and, once you become prospect-minded, you'll develop a "nose for business" just as keen as a reporter's "nose for news," or a hound dog's "nose for game." It's another way of saying that you form the habit of *paying attention*.

To fully utilize this strategy, you must constantly be on the lookout for bits of information of value to you. These surface in your office, waiting to interview a prospect, talking on the phone, at lunch, and at home listening to a conversation or reading the newspaper.

2. The endless chain strategy. This is predicated upon the theory that from each interview or each buyer you should be able to secure the names of other prospects.

In employing this strategy, attempt to get from each person interviewed information about and/or introductions to two or three of their contacts who possess the need for your product or service. Naturally, this strategy is more effective in instances where you have been successful in selling the prospect just interviewed. New buyers are generally sufficiently enthusiastic about their purchase to believe that some of their friends and contacts will likely want to consider the same proposition.

The term "endless chain" is applied to the process of securing an endless number of qualified sales links from a single source. When you employ this strategy, you can, in fact, make it a never-ending chain. Each introduction carries with it an element of recommendation. Your new prospect realizes that unless their friend had been helped by you, they would never have provided the introduction. This constitutes a "referred lead." It is the best kind of prospect, because a level of trust and common interest has been established between you and the prospect.

3. The center-of-influence strategy. In using this strategy, you develop a number of people who will serve as feeders. In some cases, these people will be customers and clients; in other instances, they may be influential friends who are willing to cooperate.

An illustration of the manner in which this strategy might be applied is the "Board of Directors" developed by the late Dick Reed, one of the life insurance industry's top performers. We watched Dick move his production from $1 million to over $25 million in a *single year* as a *direct result* of organizing his center of influence.

Dick picked 10 prominent citizens to serve on his personal "Board of Directors." Each month, he called the board together for a regular luncheon meeting. Insurance ideas were discussed and prospects were developed that propelled him into the big league in selling! It can possibly do the same for you.

When you employ the center-of-influence strategy, it is important to make an effort to repay the services of your contact group by regular reminders of appreciation and goodwill, such as gifts at Christmas, cards on important occasions and frequent calls to thank them personally for their assistance. Remember, no one is going to give much thought to helping you unless you can establish yourself as a knowledgeable professional and a skilled representative.

4. The junior associate strategy. Batman has his Robin, Holmes has his Watson and great actors and actresses have understudies. Many professional salespeople have found that there is value in having a Junior Associate. This person acts as a "bird dog" and points out contacts that the more experienced sales professional will call on and sell. *This strategy is employed in those selling situations that require both contacts and technical information.* Your "bird dog" sniffs around and locates prospects and then signals to the "experienced hunter" who brings them in. This strategy enables you to use your time more efficiently and makes it easier to "bag your limit."

5. The direct mail strategy. This strategy is used effectively for products that are bought repeatedly, especially when used in connection with previous buyers and present users.

To employ this strategy, you send a prepared announcement with the idea of calling first upon those who respond and invite you to call. Ultimately, your plan should be to get around to the rest. Frequently, direct mail makes your prospect conscious of a need not realized until the message is received.

The "lead service letters" of many companies today are excellent examples of direct mail generating live prospects who have not previously perceived any need for their product or service. As a result of a well-structured letter, recipients respond and ask that you come to see them. If they don't respond, you still have made them aware of you and your service and have a natural lead to follow up on.

6. The cold canvass strategy. This strategy assumes that you know little or nothing about the person being called upon except perhaps his or her name. The law of averages is supposed to result in a satisfactory number of good prospects and, hence, sales being developed simply through the volume of cold calls made.

Many salespeople today contend that this prospecting strategy is no strategy at all—that it lacks professionalism. *Obviously,* the nature of the product being sold has a great deal to do with the strategies you use. Cold canvass may be a sound approach to use in the sale of a generally used tangible product. It is more debatable in the case of intangible services which are sold largely on the basis of confidence and contacts. The cold canvass strategy is much better adapted to selling those products and services that are almost essential—such things as automobiles, home appliances, fire and auto insurance, since every prospect approached either needs them or will need them at some future date.

PLANNING AND PROSPECTING SUMMED UP

Nothing in selling is more important than planning and prospecting! It always pays to "plan your work and work your plan." More important than how *much* work you do is what *kind* of work you do. It's more important to "work smart" than to "work hard."

Just as you wouldn't begin a day of driving without a clear idea of where you were going, you shouldn't begin a day of selling without having prepared a "road map" to follow.

There are basically four types of salespeople: suppliers, interceptors, educators and generators. These are listed in *ascending* order, going from the easiest and least well paid to the most difficult and most profitable. While planning is necessary in all four fields, it is increasingly important as your job increases in importance.

Good planning means that you:

- subscribe to the "box time" theory,
- plan to wake up employed,
- plan a monthly self-organization day,
- and know the best kept sales secret!

Good prospecting means that you:

- learn to pay attention
- use a "tickler" system
- know the six basic prospecting strategies
    1. Personal observation
    2. Endless chain
    3. Center-of-influence
    4. Junior associate
    5. Direct mail
    6. Cold canvass

PLANNING AND PROSPECTING REMINDERS

- Planning is just as important as doing and should take place before doing.
- The daily planning of priorities provides an intelligent course of action to be followed.
- The planning discipline keeps you focused.
- Your success in selling depends, in large measure, upon your ability to recognize priorities and to stay focused on them.
- Prospecting successfully on a consistent basis boils down to paying attention.

- Prospecting is the search for needers who can be changed into wanters and then into buyers.

- The personal observation strategy calls for you to form a habit of alertness.

- An introduction to a prospect carries with it an element of endorsement.

- The junior associate strategy works best in those selling situations that recognize both contacts and technical information.

- Remember, a good prospector is almost sure to outsell the salesperson who may be strong in closing sales but who lacks prospecting skills and strategies.

CHAPTER 3

HOW THE BUYER BUYS AND HOW THE SELLER SELLS

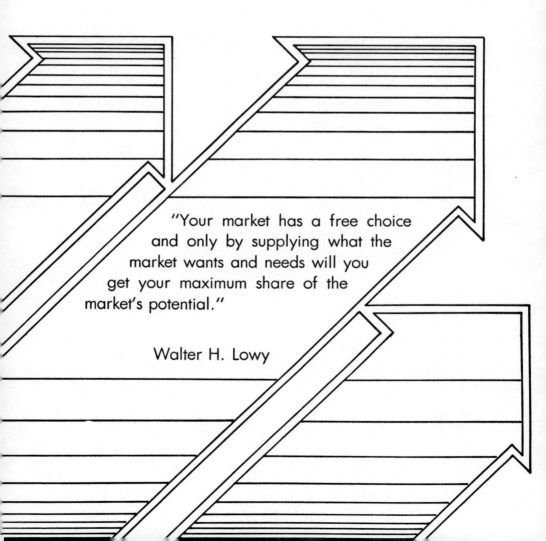

"Your market has a free choice and only by supplying what the market wants and needs will you get your maximum share of the market's potential."

Walter H. Lowy

NOTHING HAPPENS UNTIL
SOMEONE MAKES THE DECISION
TO BUY SOMETHING

This all-important buying decision is the "trigger" of the marketing cycle. Everything in a company depends on the salesperson pulling that trigger—assisting the buyer in buying. Your success, and that of your company, is tied to your skill in selling. Remember, the secret of success in selling is forming good sales habits. That means you are willing to do things failures won't do. Successful salespeople are motivated by the desire for pleasing *results*. Mediocre salespeople are influenced by the desire for pleasing *methods*.

You are a creature of habit just as a machine is a creature of momentum. *Every single qualification for success in selling is acquired by habit.* You discipline yourself to form right habits and those habits shape your future. If you do not deliberately form good habits, then unconsciously you will form bad ones.

You are, and will always be, the kind of salesperson you are because you have formed the habit of doing those things unsuccessful people don't like to do. The only way you can change yourself is by changing your habits. Habit formation and habit alteration are the result of discipline.

"Success is an inside job."

HOW SUCCESS IS EARNED

The success habits in selling which require daily discipline can be divided into five main groups.

1. thinking right
2. working right
3. selling right
4. studying right
5. living right

Let's examine each of these briefly.

1. Thinking right. *"You become what you think about most of the time."* Thinking right requires you to form the habit of thinking greatly of your function. See its significance. Consider your sales job to be most worthwhile, important and necessary. Don't sell yourself short. Make every occasion a great occasion. Remember, it's *always* too early to quit.

2. Working right. *"Honest, intelligent effort is always rewarded."* Establish the habit of starting your selling day at a specific time. Form the daily planning habit that assures you of staying focused on priority activities. Developing a regular routine permits you to accomplish much more and leads to a consistent effort.

3. Selling right. *"Be a professional client-getter—not a client-visitor."* Selling right boils down to three basic fundamentals: paying attention, staying in front of decision-makers and having a good sales strategy.

4. Studying right. *"An individual who doesn't read and digest information or learn from cassettes is no better off than one who cannot."* Long ago, you formed the habit of feeding your body regularly—remember to feed your mind too! The learning process is a continual one. You wouldn't quit eating when you turned 30 just because you had eaten regularly for the first 29 years of your life; never quit feeding your mind, either! The learning process is a continual one. Studying right means forming the habit of learning as much as possible about your product, your prospects and your performance.

5. Living right. *"You are what you repeatedly do. Excellence, then, is not an act but a habit."* Living right requires you to balance every area of your life. Success escapes many talented people because of their unwillingness or inability to develop this habit.

Success is learned best by those who learn quickly to form the habit of thinking right, working right, selling right, studying right and living right.

"Nothing builds self-confidence like successful experiences."

THE FIVE BUYING DECISIONS

Discipline comes first. Discipline builds right habits that reflect themselves in right actions. Right actions, when accompanied by strategy, always produce right results.

Let's turn to our study of selling strategy. It begins with an understanding of how the buyer buys.

You must assist the prospect in making certain decisions, one decision at a time. When your prospect has made them all, he or she has bought your product or service. How does the buyer buy? The buyer buys by making the following decisions:

- I will see and then listen to this salesperson.
- I realize and recognize a need.
- I will evaluate a possible solution to my problem.
- I approve the proposition offered. I'm convinced.
- I will act now.

These five different, important decisions must be reached in a logical, orderly manner.

STEPS IN THE SELLING PROCESS

Throughout your career, you must be learning more and better ways of assisting your prospects in making each of these buying decisions. In a sense, you play the role of "assistant buyer." To play your role effectively, you must master the five steps in the selling process.

- **Step one:** *Pre-approach*—The aim here is to get the prospect's attention. You sell the prospect on *listening* . . . giving you an appointment on a favorable basis.
- **Step two:** *Approach*—This has two chief objectives: First, to make a favorable impression. Second, to gain positive interest in learning more about your product or service.
- **Step three:** *Probing*—The primary objective of this step is to assist the prospect in *recognizing a need,* then arousing an interest in evaluating a possible solution.
- **Step four:** *Presenting*—Here you create desire by

showing the advantages now being missed that will be gained by *accepting* your sales proposition.
- **Step five:** *Closing*—Few prospects are ready to accept a sales offer even when interest has been aroused and desire has been created. You must add a closing motivation of a logical and/or emotional nature.

WANT-CREATOR VS. NEEDS-SATISFIER

Frank Bettger once said, "I am convinced the most important secret of selling is to find out what the prospect wants, then help him or her find the best way to get it."

In order to sell people effectively, you must form the habit of putting yourself in the prospect's place.

Charley McCann, a leading diesel engine salesman in Montreal for 35 years, said this to us: "The day I began to consider myself a want-creator, rather than merely a needs-satisfier, was a red letter day in my selling life."

"Do unto others as you would have them do unto you" and you will be utilizing the strongest tool yet developed for carving out a successful career in selling.

Remember, the golden rule is always golden in selling.

HOW THE BUYER BUYS AND HOW THE SELLER SELLS SUMMED UP

Remember that no one really wants to be *sold* anything—their stimulus, in their mind, comes because *they've* decided to *buy*. Until they decide to buy, nothing can happen—it's up to you to help them make that decision!

Acquire the habit of thinking right, working right, selling right, studying right and living right. Then remember that there are five steps on the ladder of decision. First, a prospect must decide to *see* and *listen,* then to recognize a *need,* then to *evaluate* your solution, then to *approve* the solution and then to act *now.* If you don't skip any rungs on the way up, your career will be on the way up too!

HOW THE BUYER BUYS AND HOW THE SELLER SELLS REMINDERS

- Nothing happens until someone makes the decision to buy something.
- Success comes to those who form the habit of doing things that failures don't like to do.
- Successful people are influenced by the desire for pleasing results, not pleasing methods.
- Habit forming and habit changing are the result of discipline.
- You become what you think about most of the time.
- Honest, intelligent effort is always rewarded in selling.
- You assist the prospect in making certain decisions—one at a time.
- The prospect must realize and recognize a need.
- The prospect must be convinced of your proposition's value and benefits.
- You play the important role of being an "assistant buyer."

- Probing arouses interest.
- Presenting creates desire.
- Most sales do not close themselves. You must add the motivation of a logical and/or emotional close.
- Be more than a needs-satisfier, be a want-creator.
- A secret of successful salesmanship is staying in front of decision-makers with a selling strategy.

CHAPTER 4

MAKING CONTACT: WINNING PRE-APPROACH STRATEGIES

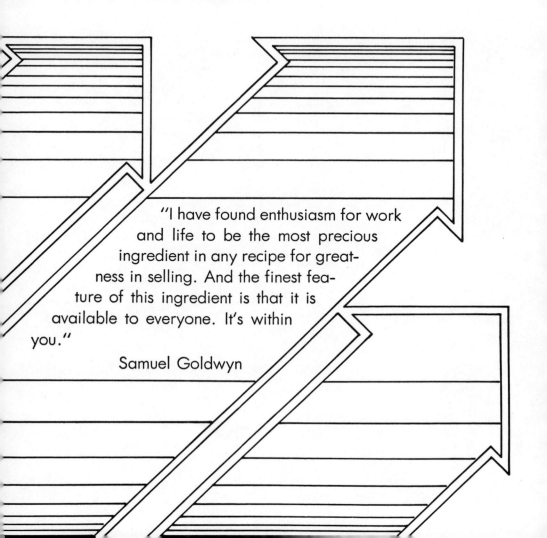

"I have found enthusiasm for work and life to be the most precious ingredient in any recipe for greatness in selling. And the finest feature of this ingredient is that it is available to everyone. It's within you."

Samuel Goldwyn

WHERE THE "BALL GAME" IS WON

Football games are won at the point of initial contact—the line of scrimmage. Sales are won at the point of initial contact—the pre-approach. Fred Novy, a great and successful salesman in Chicago, says, "Making a great many calls will do almost anything that super-salesmanship can do—and many things it can't."

People remain names on cards and only become prospects when they are contacted and interviewed under favorable conditions.

IT'S A SERIES OF DECISIONS

Again, the sale you make is always a series of decisions in favor of your proposition. Be reminded of this fundamental truth.

The purpose of your pre-approach is to assist your prospect in making the first decision—to give you an appointment under favorable circumstances. A pre-approach can be made using a telephone call, a personal visit, a letter, or a combination of these methods.

PREPARING FOR THE INITIAL CONTACT CALL

After the prospect is identified, but prior to your initial contact, you assume an important role. You become, for all practical purposes, an investigator. How extensive this kind of preparation is varies with the nature of your sales position and the kind of products you sell.

In most selling jobs, the investigative work and the subsequent use of this information can make or break the setting up of an appointment.

Sales do not just happen. Most often, they're the result of planning and the application of strategy in the "get ready" phases. The investigative work you do in preparation for the initial contact will contribute to both your effectiveness and time management.

This pre-planning is vitally important. In his days as a quarterback, Roger studied game films of the team he was to play against next. He learned their moves, their formations, their favorite plays. He tried to learn how they would respond to different approaches and circumstances. Correctly sizing up the other team *before* they came together was a vital part of the whole success story, because once the game began, they followed a pre-determined game plan on every major play!

In selling, we have all found that this same attention to detail, *before* that initial contact is made, is very, very vital to the success of the game—whether your game is football, baseball or selling!

OBJECTIVES OF PLANNING
THE INITIAL CONTACT

The following objectives of the investigative planning phase, when accomplished, will help you function at your best during your initial contact. These objectives are to:

- accumulate any special information that can help you present yourself in the strongest possible manner
- discover what the prospect's dominant buying motive will most likely be
- gain insights on how you can best establish a good relationship

To become proficient in obtaining the information you require, you must sharpen your questioning and observation skills. Generally, finding out what you want to know is a matter of asking the right people. Most people will want to help, if properly approached. Here are the important things to do:

First, seek out information about the prospect:

- Personality characteristics
- Special interest, sports and hobbies
- Family ties and marital status
- Business aims, ambitions and objectives
- Business needs
- Special personal or business problems

Second, gain information about the prospect's company:

- Comparative growth in industry
- Most pressing needs

- Specific business problems
- Experience with similar products
- Objections likely to be raised
- How they are doing now
- How your product or service will help them do better

Finally, secure an introduction and/or endorsement of you and your product or service. You gather this important information and these helpful insights in a variety of ways.

First, listen to:

- existing clients
- other salespeople
- receptionists
- assistants and secretaries
- the prospect's associates and employees

Second, read:

- local daily papers
- technical journals and trade papers
- special surveys, reports and bulletins
- magazine articles

Next, talk with:

- trade association members
- other experienced salespeople

Finally:

- Assemble your findings.
- Coordinate information and insights.
- Analyze the facts and your feelings.

THE MOST IMPORTANT THING

After you've done your homework, the next most important thing is to make the *right* contact and then *get in!*

One of America's top salesmen is Cleveland's Corwin Riley of the Kirby Company. Once we asked him what he considered the most important thing in selling and he replied with two words: *"Get in!"*

Corwin went ahead to explain how important he feels it is to assist the prospect in wanting your product or service, and how essential it is to keep your thinking right. "However, these are to no avail," he added, "if you fail to *get in!"*

To see how important this is, look at the final result you want and work backward. What is the final result you want? A satisfied client and a sales commission, of course.

> **But:**
> **You can't secure a client and collect a commission until you make a sale.**
> **You can't make the sale until you've written up the order.**
> **You can't write the order until you get an interview.**
> **And, you can't have an interview until you *get in!***

Making the contact and getting in is the foundation of success in selling.

One of the most dynamic sales organizations in the history of American business is Amway. Amway sales surpass the $1 billion mark annually. We have always felt that one of the reasons for the Amway success story lies in the philosophy professed by its co-founder and president, Rich DeVos. Here is what he has to say:

> **The most important thing in selling is selling.**
> **It is not talent, for many people with little talent make it.**
> **It is not product knowledge, for many with limited detail knowledge make it.**
> **It is not singly enthusiasm or persistence or all the other good things that make up the whole.**
> **After 30 years of watching and working with winners (and some losers), I'm convinced it all comes down to action.**
> **Nothing will take the place of doing something now.**
> **Get the body in front of the prospect and sell.**
> **That's what it's all about, and that's the pay-off point.**

Estrella Lynch is a great inspiration for women entering sales—especially those who have the feeling that it takes years of diligent study and experience to become a steady producer.

Estrella led her company, The Prudential, during her *third* year! She's a $10 million a year producer in Los Angeles!

"I tell them with my eyes that they are the most important people in my life at the time of the interview. I listen for clues to help me decide the thing that is most important in their lives. I work hard to come across to the prospect as an understanding, unhurried, conscientious agent. *I want the time the prospect spends with me to be a high spot of his or her day."*

What makes *you* feel important—that someone wants to sell you something? No, of course not. What makes you feel important is the fact that someone recognizes you as an individual, as the special person that you are. When you take time to do your homework on prospects, you're letting them know they were important enough to research.

We asked a buyer for a large Mexican restaurant chain what irritated him most about salespeople, and he replied, "When they haven't taken time to do their homework! I've had people come in and want to sell me white bread, fruit pies and all of the other things *most* restaurants use, but we don't. That tells me that we weren't even important enough for them to stop and look at one of our menus. A salesperson like that is not only wasting my time, but his—and certainly puts himself in a bad light if he *should* happen to have some products we could use!"

DON'T TELL YOUR STORY FOR THE PRACTICE

One of the most important strategies in making contact calls is to make the right one. You may have researched the contact, the company and know all there is to know about them, but if your contact doesn't have the authority to *buy,* then you're wasting your time!

If we had a dollar for every hour wasted each year by sales reps who tell their stories to the wrong person, we would be on Easy Street. It is important to see the right person *first*. The only people worth talking to are the people who have the authority to give you the order when you have convinced them that they should buy.

Trying to sell someone who does not have the authority to buy is a double mistake. First, you waste your time. Second and perhaps even worse, the individuals interviewed are apt to become obstacles because they do not want you to realize their lack of authority.

Be careful not to be fooled by titles. They are often misleading. The rule to follow is this: When in doubt, go to the top. When you start at the top, you generally get action and decisions. Often, the top person will take you to the right person and introduce you. This can be construed as "an approval from the boss."

You seldom go wrong when you start at the top. When you start too low on the ladder of authority, you are dependent upon someone else to relay your story. No one can tell your story with the power you can—so, when appropriate, eliminate the "middle person." You can't expect the buyer's assistant to do your selling for you.

The same things hold true in direct consumer selling. Whether the interview is conducted in an office, a home or a business, it is still important to talk directly to the decision-maker. In nearly every family group, there is one member who decides upon most family expenditures. Find out who the decision-maker is and direct your selling efforts toward that individual. You can increase your selling effectiveness by making sure that you tell your story in your way to the right person.

TAKE THIS PLEDGE NOW

Before you move ahead, stop and take this pledge. Feed it into your mental computer so that you can recall it instantly for the rest of your selling career.

"I will never make contact with a prospect until I have written out my script, practiced and learned my lines so that they can be expressed naturally, conversationally and sincerely."

Taking the pledge assures your effectiveness for three reasons. First, it allows you to say the right thing, not occasionally, but every time. Second, it allows you to say the right thing in the fewest possible words. Finally, it gives you confidence, because you know what you are going to say.

As Frank Sullivan says, "Ad-libs are for amateurs. In selling you must prepare much like a professional in acting—going over the lines a hundred times or more."

Many successful salespeople owe their selling success to the fact that they "took the pledge"—why not join in?

FACING THE IMPORTANT
FOUR-MINUTE BARRIER

Dr. Leonard Zunin, a Los Angeles psychiatrist, says the first four minutes of your initial contact are the crucial ones. He says, "It is the average time, demonstrated by careful observation, during which the prospect decides to continue or terminate the discussion." Dr. Zunin goes on to say, "All salespeople must be reminded they constantly face the four-minute barrier during which a favorable impression must be established."

It's human nature to make quick decisions based upon "feelings" and "hunches." *The more positive the feeling prospects have toward you, the more they will tend to hear and accept what you say.*

The following is a list of "do's" and "don'ts" to review often:

- *Do be prompt for the appointment.*
- Don't mispronounce your prospect's name.
- *Do make the object of your call clear immediately.*
- Don't show impatience.
- *Do give a warm greeting with a firm handshake.*
- Don't chew gum.
- *Do put a smile on your lips and in your voice and eyes.*
- Don't smoke, even if your prospect does.
- *Do find something to praise.*
- Don't compliment unless it's believable.
- *Do watch your posture and look your customer in the eyes.*
- Don't pull at your glasses, tap with your fingers or use other distractors.
- *Do avoid conversation relating to politics, race and religion.*
- Don't use profanity.
- *Do stay enthusiastic. It's contagious. It attracts a favorable response.*

FIVE WAYS TO COPE WITH CALL RELUCTANCE

Call reluctance will plague you throughout your career. You can learn to cope with call reluctance in five ways:

1. *Saturate yourself with positive, upbeat feelings.* This produces a commanding posture and attitude. Dorothy Sarnoff, the well-known New York City consultant, taught us a powerful attitude conditioner. Dorothy recommends feeding your mind and body with stimulants she calls "my million-dollar energizers."

   "I'm energetic, enthusiastic and effective. I'm prepared, poised and persuasive."

   With this kind of mental conditioning, you key yourself up to trigger favorable responses.

2. *Prepare yourself technically.* No matter how long a show plays on Broadway, the actors continue to study. They must know exactly what they are selling. They must understand the response and reaction that they must generate from their audience. Knowing your product and your lines gives you a competitive edge. It builds your confidence in selling the prospect.

3. *Focus on the rewards of success,* never the penalty of failure. The very next call can have results that change your entire week or month. Imagine how you'll feel after such a sale! You can never control your *feelings,* but you can control what you *imagine.* Feelings follow thought. Keep your thoughts optimistic. Act the way you want to feel.

> *"Focus on the rewards of success—not the penalties of failure."*

4. *Remember that most people are nice.* Most of the people you'll call on will be nice people—just like yourself. If you go in with a mental chip on your shoulder, thinking, "This buyer will really be tough," it will show in your attitude.

5. *Remember that most people may not show they're nice right away.* These nice people you'll be dealing with may not show their true colors during the first couple of minutes of the interview. They may be tense and nervous and act "abnormal"—as though they aren't *really* nice at all. This is even more reason for you to stay in control as a poised and prepared professional. *Let them key off your attitude—don't you key off theirs!*

To be a success, you must develop call courage. You build it in these five ways and by pumping into your bloodstream the motivational suggestion, *"Do it now!"* Psychologists teach that the surest way to develop courage is to act courageous—to do the thing you fear.

If you fear making calls, then begin making them now. Call courage can be developed. Start now!

Your Aim Is to Gain an Appointment

In making this all-important initial call, keep it concise, simple and to the point. Put yourself in the prospect's position and view your pre-approach through his or her eyes.

Never imply anything about buying your product or service during this period. In a sense, you are not trying to "sell a solution" or "sell a product" on the initial contact. Your sole aim is to "sell an appointment!"

Make the Object of Your Call Clear Immediately

Don't ask for "just a few minutes of your time" and hope to stretch it into a longer session. Ask for what you need and give your honest assurance that everything you have to offer can be described in that length of time, unless he or she *wants* more information.

Plan to Sell the Prospect on Listening

You will get your prospect's favorable attention in any one or more of these ways:

- Promise a benefit.
- Offer a service.
- Appeal to curiosity.

Never take for granted your prospect will want to listen. Instead, launch your pre-approach with reasons why he or she will want to listen.

Your pre-approach plan should be memorized and repeatedly rehearsed. It must be conversational in tone (not rote!) and instinctive if you are going to be consistently effective in setting appointments.

Practice in a small room so that you can hear yourself and improve your voice quality. Practice in front of a mirror. Put your pre-approach lines on a cassette tape to critique and improve your technique. Practicing the right lines makes for perfection. Knowing exactly what you are going to say and how you will say it gives you confidence.

Of course, the manner in which you pre-approach your prospect is important too. Make your initial contact show a poised, positive attitude. Be certain your prospect senses by your entire manner that what you have to say is important. Remember, Dr. Zunin says that relationships are made or lost in the first four minutes of that initial contact! It's important that your prospect's initial impression of you is favorable!

> *"The prospect's first attention is focused on you—not your proposition."*

Making Contact by Telephone

In many selling positions the telephone call has replaced the personal visit in making the initial contact with prospects. The telephone is the one business tool that helps budget time, qualify prospects and enhance your professional image.

The peculiar advantages of the telephone are:

- The number of calls can be increased.
- Cost per call is reduced.
- Effectiveness may be improved. It is often possible to gain the ear of a busy prospect when you couldn't gain a face-to-face interview.
- Brevity is encouraged. It encourages concentration on both ends of the wire.
- You can work rapidly over the telephone and concentrate your personal calls on large buyers or those who require a visit.
- Opportunity is provided for you to obtain an immediate decision.

Ken Miller at Phoenix says, "In my business, 10 cold sales calls resulting in one appointment can take a *full day*. Ten phone calls resulting in one appointment takes only one hour." This is quite an advantage when you are measuring time investment versus return.

Telephone contacts have their weaknesses too:

- The opportunity to present a complete message is often lacking.
- Some regard the telephone as an intruder.
- Appeal is to the sense of hearing only. You can't show samples, use visual aids, or impress with your personal appearance.
- It's easier to say "No" over the telephone.

Basic Telephone Strategies to Employ

The situation requires you to develop telephone effectiveness. You'll find it helpful to review these basic strategies often.

1. Choose a private spot to make your calls and avoid any interruption.
2. Build and use a script. Know exactly what you are going to say before you call.
3. Introduce yourself and your company, and state the purpose of your call quickly.
4. Verify the name of the prospect to whom you are speaking. Make sure of its pronunciation. Use the prospect's name frequently.
5. Courtesy, sincerity and clarity of speech are essential to your success. Use "thank you," "may I ask" and other expressions that demonstrate good manners. Put a smile in your voice. A mirror in front of you helps you smile.
6. Be aggressive without seeming to be so. Using questions that invite "yes" answers is the best

strategy for driving through without giving your prospect the opportunity to cut off the conversation.

7. By all means, avoid an argument. No matter what the response from the prospect is, ask for the appointment—give the prospect a choice.

8. Sell your name. Ask the prospect to write it down.

9. Take frequent breaks if you are calling over an extended period of time. Telephone calling is an exhausting activity.

10. Thank your prospect and always let the prospect hang up first.

Whether your pre-approach is made in person, by telephone or letter is usually dictated by the situation (your territory, the nature of your product or service, local business customs and other pertinent factors). However, the theme remains consistent. Many of the words will be identical. The objective is always the same—gaining an appointment.

RECOMMENDED TIMES TO TELEPHONE	
Accountants	April 16 to December 31
Attorneys	11 am to 2 pm; 4 to 5 pm
Bankers	Before 10 am; after 3 pm
Builders	Before 8 am; after 5 pm
Business Owners	Between 10:30 am and 3 pm
Clergy	Between Tuesday and Friday
Dentists	Between 8:30 am and 9:30 pm
Druggists	Between 1 pm and 3 pm
Engineers/Chemists	Between 4 pm and 5 pm
Executives	Before 8:30 am; after 4 pm
Homemakers	Midmorning; Midafternoon

Manufacturers	Between 10:30 am and 3 pm
Physicians	Before 9:30 am; after 4:30 pm
Retail Merchants	Between 1 pm and 3 pm
Sales Managers	Afternoons
Salespeople	Weekends
Stockbrokers	Before 10 am; after 3 pm
Professors and Teachers	After 4:30 on weekdays; anytime on weekends or holidays

Working customs in your locality may vary but these are generally effective guidelines.

One other good idea relative to the telephone comes from Jay Lewis, a top producer in Chicago. "I started reaching and surpassing my goals the day I made the decision to install a toll free number," Jay says. "I put in a toll free line at a cost of $40 per month and it increased my earnings $2,000 a month almost immediately."

CRUCIAL FACTORS

Selling successfully is generally based on two fundamental activities:

- Consistently obtaining a sufficient number of qualified prospects
- Contacting these people in a manner which leads to them granting you an appointment

The foundation for selling success lies in getting interviews. The secret of getting good, attentive interviews is in setting appointments. That's why we say the pre-approach, the selling of an appointment, is the crucial factor in selling success.

When carefully planned pre-approaches are made to a sufficient number of prospects each week, enough interviews will be arranged and enough sales produced to reach your personal objectives. It's as simple as that! Honest, intelligent effort is always rewarded—and it all starts by making the contact call correctly!

MAKING CONTACT SUMMED UP

The first rule of selling is, *"Get in."* If you don't get in, it doesn't matter how good your presentation, how good your product, or how superior the service is that you offer.

You can't score if you're not on the field during the game—and you can't score in selling if you aren't where the prospects are!

You *get in* by planning, by learning as much as you can about your prospect and your prospect's company. You're not merely looking for idle chit-chat items, you're looking for "handles" that might help you motivate the prospect.

Knowledge and an appointment alone won't sell the prospect. You can't score unless you're playing in the right ballpark. You can't sell unless your prospect has the *authority to buy*. If you aren't certain, *ask!* Say, "Pardon me, Mr. Wilson, but are you the person with the authority to buy running boards here at the Antique Refinishers Corporation? Oh, you're *not?* Then perhaps I should see Mr. Johnson instead, so that I won't waste *your* time."

Don't tell your story for the practice—tell it where it'll do some good!

Once you've got the appointment made, be prompt, polite, personable, posture-perfect, poised and persuasive. That's a mouth full of "p's" that add up to "profits!"

A tightrope walker doesn't look down at how long the drop is or how narrow the rope. He or she looks steadily at the goal—the other side. Don't *you* concentrate on the penalties of failure—fasten your mind on the rewards of success. As the old song goes, "You gotta accentuate the positive, eliminate the negative, don't mess with Mr. In-Between!"

If you keep your mind positive, you'll remember that most people are nice—just like you. It may just take them a few minutes to show it.

Learn how to make the telephone work for you. Make a well-written, well-rehearsed telephone presentation part of your success story.

Finally, learn the best times to call. However, a call at almost *any* time is better than no call at all. After all, remember:

> **You can't collect a commission until you make a sale. You can't make the sale until you've written up the order. You can't write up the order until you get an interview. And you can't have an interview if you don't *get in!***

MAKING CONTACT REMINDERS

- Sales are won at the point of contact.
- The sale of your product or service is always a series of sales.
- The purpose of your pre-approach is to sell an appointment.

- One of the advantages of using the telephone is that it encourages brevity.

- A disadvantage of the telephone is that it appeals to one sense only.

- When calling, introduce yourself and your company, and state your purpose quickly.

- Clarity of speech, sincerity and courtesy are essential to your success on the telephone.

- As you plan your pre-approach, you want to gain insights on how you can best establish a good relationship.

- Also, you want to learn as much as possible about the prospect's buying habits.

- Secure an introduction whenever possible. It builds credibility.

- "Taking the pledge" assures you of speaking conversationally.

- Be prompt for the appointment.

- Make the object of your call clear immediately.

- Don't compliment unless it is believable.

- The prospect can be expected to act "abnormally" during the early minutes.

- Stay enthusiastic; it's contagious.

- On the initial contact, you are not trying to sell a solution.

- You get the prospect's favorable attention when you promise a benefit, offer a service and/or appeal to curiosity.

- Be certain the prospect always recognizes that what you have to say is important.

CHAPTER 5

PROBING:
HOW TO GAIN
POSITIVE INTEREST
IN YOUR PRODUCT

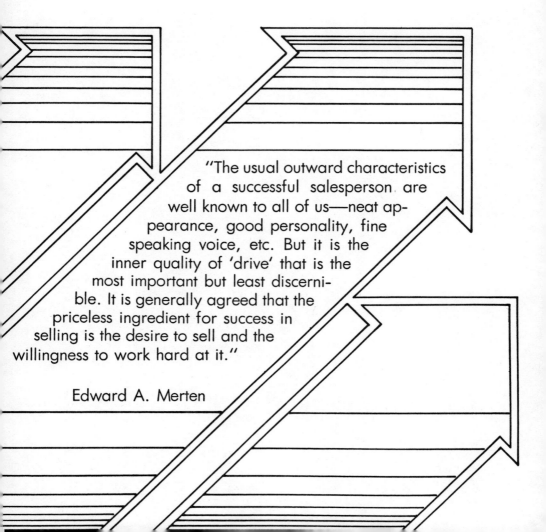

"The usual outward characteristics of a successful salesperson are well known to all of us—neat appearance, good personality, fine speaking voice, etc. But it is the inner quality of 'drive' that is the most important but least discernible. It is generally agreed that the priceless ingredient for success in selling is the desire to sell and the willingness to work hard at it."

Edward A. Merten

THE APPROACH AND ITS OBJECTIVES

Selling is leading your prospect to make certain decisions, one decision at a time. A most important decision has already been made—the decision to grant you an appointment. The prospect has made that decision; you have made the first in a series of sales you'll have to make before you're ready to write up the order.

The *approach* is the name given to the second stage of the selling process, presumably because it is the first actual meeting between you and your prospect. The approach has two chief objectives:

- To make a favorable impression upon the prospect and secure favorable attention
- To gain positive interest in the product or service you came to talk about

During the approach, build an atmosphere of trust so that your prospect will be open to your ideas. Get your prospect to listen. Condition the prospect to logically consider your service, your product and your recommendation.

PROBING—ITS OBJECTIVES

Robert Hutchins, when Chancellor at the University of Chicago, said, "One of the biggest things you get out of a college education is a questioning attitude, a habit of developing and weighing evidence—a scientific approach." The objective of probing is to assist the prospect in making two important decisions:

- To recognize a need
- To become interested in evaluating a possible solution

The best way to get your prospect to think and recognize a need is to ask questions—*relevant* questions. In many cases, it's the only way you will get the prospect to think.

People do not buy something unless they feel it is in their interest and benefit to do so. The "interest" may be on the part of themselves, their family, their company, their charity or their community. The point to remember is that probing questions provide you with pertinent information.

One of the surest ways to increase your selling effectiveness is to learn more about what your prospects want. Strategic questions develop this kind of information.

PROBING—ITS ADVANTAGES

There are a number of things you gain by developing a questioning strategy:

- It helps your prospect discover a need.
- It helps you avoid talking too much.
- It helps avoid arguments.

- It helps crystallize the prospect's thinking—the idea becomes his or hers.
- It helps give your prospect a feeling of importance when you show respect for his or her opinions; he or she is more likely to respect your opinions and recommendations.

KNOW WHERE THE SALE IS MADE

A sale is not made in your mind or over the counter, but in the mind of your prospect. Every word, every question, every gesture you make during the first face-to-face meeting should have only one objective: assisting the prospect in discovering a need.

This is merely another way of saying you must cultivate the habit of viewing yourself and your acts through the eyes of your prospect. This habit makes you a more agreeable person and more highly regarded as a friend. It assures you of making more sales.

LEARNING IS LISTENING

Learning about your prospect and his or her needs is largely a listening process. *Learn to listen. Listen to learn.*

Listening wins favorable attention. It helps you focus on the needs of your prospect as revealed in the answers to your questions.

Effective listening habits include the following:

- *Stop talking*—You can't listen if you're talking.
- *Show your interest*—Look and act interested.

- *Empathize*—Put yourself in your prospect's shoes.
- *Put the prospect at ease*—Help the prospect find it easy to answer your questions.
- *Never interrupt*—Let your prospect interrupt you, but never interrupt the prospect or complete his or her sentences.

It's imperative for you to show your prospect that you are genuinely interested in his or her situation. You assist the prospect in recognizing a need and in evaluating a possible solution for that need. The key, of course, to the prospect making these two decisions in your favor lies in the quality of your probing and listening.

"Prospects don't care how much you know—they want to know how much you care."

Shirley Meyer is a national sales leader for the Metropolitan Life Insurance Company at Eugene, Oregon. Shirley is a student and a listener. Shirley's market is the logging industry. "I started by talking to the log truck drivers. I gathered all the information about them I could, including their problems. I *researched* all of their government, group and personal insurance. I rode in a log truck to the loading ramps—up and down the mountains on old logging roads. I studied to know everything possible about their business and personal insurance needs. I found out where they spent their money, how they spent it and why. Because I learned everything about their business, I gained their confidence and built an important rapport. *I listened to them—in turn they listened to me and acted on my recommendations.*"

Shirley was a participant in one of our Portland Sales

Clinics. She told the salespeople in attendance, "What it comes down to and what I truly believe is that *it is not what you know about your business that makes the sale, it is what you know about the prospect's business!"*

"Good listeners generally make more sales than good talkers."

FINDING THE FACTS

The right questions to ask depend upon the product or service you sell.

You will want to ask yourself what kind of information you must develop to prepare for your presentation.

- What specific need is recognized?
- To what degree is price a factor?
- What is the potential volume?
- Who is the decision-maker?
- What is the buying philosophy?
- How is the competition rated?

Ask confidence-building questions. These open your prospect's mind to possible needs. Examples would be, "Did you know more than 5,000 companies now use this service?" or, "Did you know we now provide an international service?"

Ask questions that will help you later key your presentation to your prospect's specific needs. You'll find that you'll get more favorable attention.

Ask questions that emphasize the benefits you offer. This technique can be learned easily. Instead of generalizing by saying, "We can bring you more profit," emphasize the specific benefits you offer. Then sum them up by saying, "As you can see, the bottom line means more profit for you."

Learn to put benefits in the form of questions. For example, few prospects would fail to show interest if you asked, "Would you be interested if we could show you how to improve your safety record and reduce your insurance costs?"

Ask questions that encourage your prospect to take an active part in the interview. Many times it's easier and more effective to gain understanding through the prospect's eyes and hands. "Can you *feel* the difference?" "Can you *see* our superior workmanship?" *"Taste* it—don't you agree it's delicious?"

Master the questioning technique to assist prospects in making the decision to study your proposition.

DISCOVER THE DOMINANT BUYING MOTIVE

Behind every purchase is a buying motive. You can test the validity of this claim from your own experience as a buyer. What caused you to buy your last car? Last TV? Last book? Last dress or suit? Perhaps you had several reasons or motives for each purchase— but *one* was the *dominant* motive, wasn't it?

There are six basic motives which move your prospect to action:

- Desire for money gain (profit)
- Fear of loss (security)
- Pride of ownership (status)
- Interest in doing it easier (efficiency)

- Desire for excitement (pleasure)
- Interest in self-improvement (effectiveness)

Buying motives vary among individuals and products. Some of them are fairly obvious. For example, a merchant who buys a new line of merchandise is motivated by the desire for profit. The individual who buys an accident policy is motivated by fear of losing security. A young person who buys a new sports car may *say* that he or she is buying it because it's needed. Actually, it is probably his or her vanity or pride of ownership at work.

So it is with everything that is bought from you. You appeal to the right motive or motives. As the old saying goes, "Everyone has two reasons for doing something—the *real reason* and one that sounds good." You need to discover the *real* reason behind each potential purchase.

Speaking of dominant buying motives, Baltasar Gracian wrote in his book *The Art of Worldly Wisdom,* published in 1653, "First guess a man's ruling passion, appeal to it by word, set it in motion by temptation, and you will infallibly give checkmate to his freedom of will. Find out each man's thumbscrew. You must know where to get at anyone. All men are idolaters; some of fame, others of self-interest, most of pleasure. Skill consists in knowing these idols in order to bring them into play. Knowing any man's mainspring of motive well, you have, as it were, the key to his will."

How do you find a prospect's dominant motive? *By asking a lot of questions—and doing a lot of careful listening!* Ask yourself what you would do and how you would react if you were the prospect. Probe well enough and long enough to get inside the prospect's mind with your questions.

When you decide on the main buying motive, be sure to record it. Don't overlook secondary or minor motives. These six forces are what motivate prospects to buy. Learn to discover the motive most likely to move each prospect to buy. Throughout your presentation, learn to concentrate on the key motive, or motives, much as a boxer concentrates on landing the perfect jab.

Each of us could give you thousands of examples of how probing on our parts enabled us to read the prospects' minds and make the sale. But probably you'll remember this example best:

It is the Superbowl game of 1978, the Dallas Cowboys versus the Denver Broncos. Each team has "probed" the other well—studied their game films, learning not only their plays, but their tendencies. From this probing, Roger has learned that Bernard Jackson, the Broncos' weak safety, tends to watch the quarterback's eyes and fade where he's looking.

The Cowboys set up a play to go to the fullback on the right side. Roger fades back to pass and looks to the right. Bernard Jackson begins running in that direction. But Roger had told Butch Johnson that instead of running end route he should go ahead and run post, and he gets behind Bernard Jackson. Roger lays the pass over Jackson's head and Johnson catches it— touchdown!

You'll score time after time if you take the time to study your prospect's "game plan" and tendencies!

PROBING SUMMED UP

The purpose of probing is to find out enough about your prospect and your prospect's situation to enable you to make intelligent recommendations. You are searching for facts and feelings that will be helpful to you in making a sale.

Your primary objective is to assist your prospect in making two important decisions:

- To recognize a need
- To become interested in evaluating a solution

When you ask questions, you develop additional facts and feelings such as:

- Understanding the prospect better as a person
- Understanding the prospect's needs as they're related to your product or service
- Understanding why it is important for the prospect to meet these needs
- Strengthening your relationship with the prospect
- Creating a more professional image
- Determining the prospect's buying power
- Determining whether the prospect is the decision-maker
- Establishing or reinforcing the prospect's decision to move forward
- Triggering in the prospect's mind mental images of what it would be like to solve the problem
- Determining the prospect's dominant buying motive

Many a prospect, thoroughly persuaded that he or she has a need, still does not buy. They are persuaded, but not convinced.

In the next chapter, you will discover presentation techniques that can bring about a state of mind that will condition your prospects for the close.

PROBING REMINDERS

- A chief objective of your approach is to make a favorable impression.
- During the approach, build an atmosphere of trust.
- Assist the prospect in recognizing a need.
- Arouse the prospect's interest in evaluating a possible solution.
- The sale must always be made in the mind of the prospect.
- Learn to listen and listen to learn.
- An important listening habit to cultivate is to never interrupt.
- Good listeners make more sales than good talkers.
- Ask questions that emphasize the benefits you can offer.
- Discover the dominant buying motive.
- Determine who the decision-maker is.
- Work hard to strengthen your relationship with each prospect.

CHAPTER 6

PRESENTATIONS THAT HELP THE PROSPECT BUY WITH CONFIDENCE

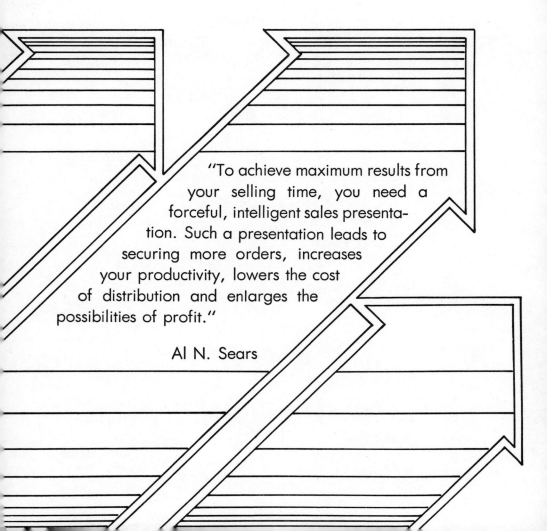

"To achieve maximum results from your selling time, you need a forceful, intelligent sales presentation. Such a presentation leads to securing more orders, increases your productivity, lowers the cost of distribution and enlarges the possibilities of profit."

Al N. Sears

WHAT A GOOD PRESENTATION MUST DO

Many salespeople owe their six-figure incomes to the fact that they prepare and present their sales talks with maximum impact. *Your presentation must be believed, agreed with and acted upon. It must be designed from the buyer's point of view.* In other words, it must give the kind of information your prospect wants and needs to have before he or she is willing to buy.

Knowing how to develop and deliver a convincing presentation is one of the surest and quickest ways for you to reach the top in selling.

> *"Every successful sales interview begins with a well-planned presentation."*

FOUR ESSENTIALS OF A GOOD PRESENTATION

Your company may have given you a prepared sales script and insisted that you learn to give it verbatim.

At the other extreme, there are firms that leave it up to you to plan and develop your own sales talk.

Whatever the practice of your company, it is necessary for you to thoroughly understand the four essentials of a result-producing presentation. No matter what your presentation is designed to sell, it must meet these four requirements if you are to sell successfully.

- It must capture the prospect's instant and undivided attention.
- It must arouse interest by describing buyer benefits and their advantages to the prospect.
- It must create desire by winning the prospect's confidence.
- It must motivate the prospect to take action *now*.

HOW TO GAIN INSTANT ATTENTION

The first requirement is unquestionably the most important. Get instant and undivided attention. Unless your prospect hears what you say, you cannot expect to get satisfactory results, no matter how well you know your lines. Your presentation, right away, must gain attention. It's not always easy to gain attention. Your prospects are not exactly waiting with bated breath for you to make your presentation. To get and hold attention, you must earn it.

How do you do it? There are two ways. One is to appeal to the senses—sight, touch, taste, hearing and smell. *"See* the superior workmanship." "You can *feel* the difference." *"Taste* it, it's delicious!" The second way to capture attention is to say or do something that relates the prospect's needs to your product or service. "We can show you how to have a better safety record and reduce your insurance rates as much as 20 percent." "We can reduce costly turnover the very first year." "Your overhead expenses will be cut in half—immediately!" *Remember, there are two reliable ways to gain attention:*

- Get the prospect into the act.
- Dramatize the value of the product or service.

In dealing with one or more people who make buying decisions, we have found the use of visuals in the form of original and creatively prepared transparencies or 35 millimeter slides to be very effective.

Here's what Bill Harmelin, a master salesman in New York City, has to say about this type of aid: "In talking to prospects without the use of these aids, frequently they will accept telephone calls or permit other interruptions; whereas my experience has been that one has their undivided attention when using transparencies or slides. I have very successful businesspeople listen for as long as 3½ hours uninterrupted. The slides or transparencies have a kind of hypnotic effect which is not present without such aids."

It is impossible to know how many sales we lose because we cannot hold the prospect's attention.

Bill Harmelin goes ahead to say: "When one uses visuals of the type described above, prospects are willing to spend more time with the salesperson and are less inclined to permit anything to interrupt the discussion. In one instance, a business prospect's secretary came in to say, 'The man with whom you have your next appointment is here.' The businessman said, 'Let him wait!' Such things never happened to me before I started to use transparencies and/or slides."

Bill concludes: "My investment in the equipment, which is available at any audiovisual supply house, came to about $600. It paid for itself after the first sale. The equipment consists of a portable overhead projector, which can be plugged into any outlet, and a transparency maker which is easy to use. There's no need to carry a screen because the projector can show clear images on any light wall."

HOW TO AROUSE INTEREST

Converting attention to favorable interest comes next. The big question you must always answer in your presentation is, "What's in this for me?" Benefits are what prospects buy. You must know which benefits will get the greatest response from your prospect.

You must ask yourself, "What is it this prospect wants or needs that is best satisfied from my proposition? What are the owner benefits he or she will buy?"

There are two types of benefits—plus benefits and minus benefits. The plus benefits are those your prospect gains through buying financial, physical, mental, social, emotional or spiritual improvements. The minus benefits are the risks or losses he or she avoids by buying from you, such as financial loss, loss of health, or loss of prestige.

You arouse interest by focusing on the owner benefits that appeal to your prospect and that he or she will buy.

"Your presentation produces orders when it is built around buyer benefits."

HOW TO CREATE DESIRE

The sale is seldom closed unless your prospect has a degree of confidence in your proposition. This confidence may depend upon your product or service, your company or you.

The colorful, capable Ralph Carlisle of Lexington, Kentucky, said to us, "One statement in a sales presentation which your prospect finds reason to doubt is like a single drop of ink in a glass of water—it colors the entire contents!"

The winning of the prospect's confidence is a vital part of your presentation. One reason: the prospect has been taught, perhaps by experience, that you can't believe everything you hear, especially when you hear it from someone who is selling.

Roger began selling shortly after he joined the Dallas Cowboy football team in 1969. In the early seasons, he was relatively unknown so that the name didn't help him get interviews. On the other hand, once the prospect found out he was a professional football player this sometimes worked against him. The buyer thought, "What can *he* know? He's really just an off-season football player." This meant that Roger had to work extra hard to win each buyer's confidence!

You, too, have to win each buyer's confidence. Frankly, the *better* the offer, the more skeptical they'll be! In order to win their confidence you must be mindful of two things:

- *First, the winning of the buyer's confidence is of no avail unless he or she has been made to want your product or service first.* Your prospect may be convinced that your product is the finest of its kind, but still not buy until and unless he or she has been made to see the need for the product and to want it. It is the *want* that makes people buy. A person may need a computer and yet may not want it because he or she doesn't know what it will do for the business. That person will not buy until he or she wants it, even though the need may have existed for some time. On the other hand, how often have you watched people buy something they do not actually need, just because they wanted it? *Your job is to arouse a sense of want before you spend too much time gaining confidence.*

* *Second, spend only as much time as is needed in the winning of confidence.* Too many facts, figures, charts and proofs of various kinds may bore a busy prospect and a bored prospect begins to lose interest.

> *"The best way to convince a buyer is to make it his or her idea."*

HOW TO GAIN THE BUYER'S CONFIDENCE

Paul Hutsey of Pittsburg, Kansas, says the key thing to develop today in sales is not salesmanship but "buymanship." We believe Paul is exactly right. Today, you must learn to function as an assistant buyer. You must demonstrate your knowledge of "buymanship" skills.

You apply "buymanship" skills in the following ways:

* *Use of testimonials.* This is based on the principle that a satisfied customer is your best single advertisement.

In advertising, testimonials are used to gain attention rather than create desire. We listen to well-known personalities like Roger on television as they promote certain products and services. In selling, you introduce the testimonial for the purpose of inspiring confidence. Your testimony will carry more weight when the individual is known to the prospect and is known to be reliable.

Testimonials in a sales presentation are best used when selling to a relatively inexperienced prospect. He or she relies heavily on the experience of others. Often, experienced buyers are not all that impressed with testimonials. They feel competent to make their own choices.

- *Speak the prospect's language.* Being able to speak the language of your prospect is one of the best ways to gain his or her confidence. The natural tendency is to speak in the jargon of your particular industry—avoid that—speak the *prospect's* language.

  Remember the "KISS" principle—Keep It Simple, Stupid!—don't try to impress a prospect with your command of your industry's jargon or the result of your latest reading of the dictionary.

- *Research results and evidence.* This method includes test results, reports from authorities and/or product sample approval by a well-known governing body. The bigger the name of the person or organization developing the evidence, the more believable the proof.

- *Guarantee.* This is a convincing sales aid, particularly when selling a new product. It is always a big advantage when you can tell your prospect that what you are selling is so good it will be guaranteed.

- *Company reputation.* This talking point carries a lot of strength when your firm has earned a reputation for quality products and superior service. Sales reps for such companies need to spend little time convincing their prospects that their product claims are true.

> *"Produce in your prospect the confidence to buy."*

HOW TO MOTIVATE TO ACTION

This is the aim of every presentation you make. The single most important attitude for you to carry into this final step is this one:

> **"I will take the initiative and assist my prospect in making the buying decision. The prospect will seldom ever close the sale. *I* must supply the motivation."**

It is vital for you to have a well-organized procedure for providing the motivation on the part of your prospect to act on your proposition *now*.

Professional selling dictates that you start the motivation by summarizing the key buyer benefits. Remind your prospect of the reasons he or she should act now. Frequently, the prospect forgets some of the reasons for buying. Your summation recalls to the prospect's mind the important things that dictate acceptance of your proposition. *Remember, one of the best ways to convert desire into action is to present the key buyer benefits in rapid-fire summation.*

It's like the elderly minister who explained that the secret of his powerful sermons was this: "First, I tell them what I'm going to tell them. Second, I tell them.

Third, I quickly tell them what I told them." Don't rely on the prospects to remember all the key points of the presentation—act as assistant buyer and remind them!

Next, ask for any questions the prospect wants answered. Assuming you have answered your prospect's questions, you should then move to questions of your own. Your strategic questions should assist the buyer in making minor decisions in favor of your proposition. These minor decisions should direct the buyer to make the important decision to buy from you now.

We like a little children's book by Dr. Seuss called *Green Eggs and Ham.* In this book, a wacky character is trying to get someone to try green eggs and ham. Obviously, the prospect isn't the least bit interested, but the salesman is persistent and begins asking questions like, "Would you like them *here* or *there*? Would you like them in a house? Would you like them with a mouse?" You might want to read this little book because in the end persistence pays off and the prospect not only tries the product but loves the product. More than that, he *appreciates* the salesman's taking time to act as assistant buyer. He is sincerely thankful.

We mention this because, after you have done all of the rest, it is now time to *ask for the order.*

"Assume the prospect is going to buy from you now."

Many buyers say it is amazing how many sales reps seem unable to bring themselves to ask for the order. Keep constantly in mind that you may have to ask the prospect for the order several times before the order is obtained.

The important thing is having an established strategy—a strategy that enables you to effectively function as an assistant buyer in motivating prospects to action; a strategy you employ with any type of prospect; a strategy you use with confidence because you know it will be result-producing.

PRESENTATION POINTERS

The stronger your presentation, the more sales you'll make. *An effective presentation is always a planned presentation.* It is planned and developed to fit your particular product or service and your prospects.

Review these presentation pointers often:

- *Personalize your presentation.* Make it tailormade. You will have a much more receptive listener.

- *Review the minutes.* Before you begin your presentation, review everything that has been previously discussed. Tell the prospect what you intend to show.

- *Plan to get your prospect involved.* The best presentations are those that give the prospect an active part. You can always manage to give your prospect an active role, no matter what you sell.

- *Slant your presentation to your prospect's self-interest.* Your presentation produces orders when it is built around buyer benefits. Jim Beveridge, a well-known marketing consultant for the defense industry, says, "Everyone feels a little bit confused, a little bit incompetent and a little bit insecure. Your presentation, while never stating these things, should show the prospect how purchasing your product or service will make them feel less confused, less incompetent and less insecure. It's natural someone would want a product or service like that."

- *Choose impact words.* Words and expressions are the raw materials out of which you construct your sales presentation. Some can trigger emotion. They cause immediate action. Some words almost automatically have impact, no matter how they are used.

As a professional, you should become a student of words. No matter what product you wish to describe, there are image-making words that will stir your prospect's imagination. Discover these words. Put them into sentences that will show them off to their best advantage.

Our study of words tells us your list of impact words should include the following:

Let's	Discovery	Wealth
Guaranteed	Proven	Please
Flexible	Secure	You
Why	Scientific	Safety
Must	Time-Saving	Positive
Help	Economical	Health
Loss	Quality	Value
Advantage	Courtesy	Popular
Easy	Status	Excel
Wise People	Up-to-Date	Sympathy
Truth	Tested	Necessary
Fitness	Tasteful	Growth
Death	Thank You	Recommended
Life	Home	Durable
Profit	Beauty	Modern

How many of these words can you tie to the sale of your product?

In addition, use "agreement," not "contract." Use "invest," not "buy." Use "arrange," not "pay." It may sound strange, but it *is* true that certain words have positive power—and other words have negative power.

Certain words and phrases can have a negative effect on your prospects. You will want to eliminate these from your selling vocabulary. Always avoid profanity and slang even if used by your prospect. "Do you understand?" and "Do you follow me?" are expressions to be eliminated. Prospects do not appreciate the implication that they are incapable of following your line of thought. Stay away from the word "obviously"—it might not be so obvious to the prospect. The word "deal" has a negative connotation with most prospects (although it is acceptable in selling real estate). Most prospects today are offended by the salesperson who starts sentences with "honestly" or "truthfully" or "believe me." Also, you will want to regularly check your selling style to eliminate distractors such as "you know?" and "Do you see what I mean?" These can become habit forming and will distract from even the most persuasive sales talk.

- *Gain understanding.* The confused prospect seldom buys. Keep it simple. Your aim is to show the prospect what your product can do for him or her. Tell the prospect what it does—not what it is. You sell the product of your product.

The great real estate salesman, Hank Dickerson, once told us, "If you can't write your idea on the back of my calling card, you don't have a clear idea of what you are selling."

- *Stop—look—listen.* Fish for feedback. Give your prospect many chances to express himself or herself. This is your opportunity to learn how the prospect reacts to your presentation.

"TALK LESS–
DEMONSTRATE MORE"

Let the prospect interrupt you, but never interrupt the prospect. Know who you are selling. Prospects react and buy differently. When interrupted, start all over again. Should you be interrupted by another individual, make the appropriate introductions. Quickly determine the interest of the new party. If it is important to do so, do not hesitate to terminate the interview and reschedule. In all likelihood, this will strengthen your case by placing the prospect under further obligation. However, if you decide to continue, it is imperative that you start all over again. Go back to the beginning and bring everyone up to the same point.

- *Achieve credibility.* Bring on your evidence and testimonials.

- *Help your prospect sell himself or herself.* The best way to convince the buyer is to make it his or her idea.

- *Use emotion and logic.* The strongest appeals are to the emotions rather than to the mind. However, the ideal presentation is a composite of appeals to the head as well as to the heart. Almost every prospect wants to be, or at least appears to be, rational in arriving at the decision to give you the order.

- *Summarize strategically.* Remind your prospect of the reasons he or she should buy now.

- *Be an assistant buyer.* Build the trust level and

then assist the prospect in taking action on your tailor-made proposition.

- *Ask the prospect to buy.* Be prepared to ask more than once.
- *Powerful presentation expressions to use.*
  - "I would appreciate *your courtesy* in giving me the time to explain our service."
  - "I want to *make certain I understand* how you feel."
  - *"May I ask* why you feel that way?"
  - "I would like very much for you to buy from me and my company. We're in a position to do a good job for you."
  - *"In addition to that,* is there any other reason for not moving forward on this matter now?"
  - *"Let's* move forward on this basis."
  - "Now here is what *I would like to do.*"
  - "I would like very much for you to *help me.*"

Learn to use these expressions in your presentations. They are confidence-builders and resistance-chasers! They will boost your effectiveness greatly.

ONLY THE BEST IS GOOD ENOUGH

The motto of a prominent Chicago advertising agency reads, "Where only the best is good enough." What a motto this would be for you to "carry into" each presentation you make. Why not adopt it as yours? Display it in your office. Carry it with you in your wallet. Weave it into the texture of everything you do and your presentation is sure to become what you want it to be—a masterpiece.

There is an indescribable superiority added to the character and fiber of the salesperson who consciously puts the trademark of quality on his or her presentation. The mental and moral effect of doing things accurately, painstakingly and thoroughly can hardly be estimated because the processes are so gradual, so subtle. Every time you obey the inward law of doing right you hear an inward approval. On the contrary, every half-done, careless, slipshod job that goes out of your hands leaves its trace of demoralization behind and excellence becomes impossible. You will like yourself much better when you have the approval of your conscience.

There is no other advertisement for the professional salesperson like a good reputation. Many of America's greatest manufacturers have regarded their reputation as their most precious possession, and under no circumstances would they allow their names to be put on an imperfect article. When Ben Hogan was trying to create a golf equipment manufacturing company back in 1953, he lovingly did each operation by himself, trying to make a set of golf clubs as near perfect as he could make them. In spite of advice from friends to go ahead and put a product Ben felt was inferior on the market, he destroyed $150,000 worth of golf clubs before he perfected his operation enough to put his *reputation* on each club!

Never allow *your* name to appear in connection with an imperfect article and success is yours. Large sums of money are often paid for the use of a name because of its reputation for integrity, reliability and excellence. Your presentations are opportunities to build this sort of a reputation.

Your Life magazine said this when talking about Walter Hoving, the retired president of Lord and Taylor and the youngest department store president in New York City: "Walter Hoving took the trouble to know many hundred times as much about his product as he would ever use in a sales talk. Perhaps that is one reason why he became top man at Bonwit Teller's and Tiffany's in New York City." Take *time* to know your product.

There is nothing like being in love with excellence. No other characteristic makes such a strong, lasting impression upon prospects. When it comes to your sales presentation, never be satisfied with "pretty good" or "that's going to be O.K., I think." Accept nothing but your best every time. Someone is watching. Someone will notice . . . and that someone may become a valuable customer.

In Italy during the early part of the eighteenth century, Stradivari put his stamp of excellence on the violins he "made for eternity." His workmanship was superior. Not one of his violins was ever known to break. Stradivari did not need any patent on his violins because no other violin maker would pay his price for excellence. Every Stradivarius in existence is still worth thousands of dollars.

In selling, you can make your own "Stradivarius." Every sales presentation can bear your personal trade-mark of excellence. Never has the demand been stronger, the supply shorter or the rewards greater!

PRESENTING SUMMED UP

If your presentation is to be believed, agreed with and acted upon, it must be designed and presented from the buyer's point of view. The *only* benefits the buyer is interested in are benefits to him or her. To be successful you must capture your prospect's instant attention, arouse his or her interest by describing benefits, create desire through winning confidence, and motivate the buyer to take action *now.*

You gain attention by appealing to the senses or by relating your product to your prospect's needs.

You arouse interest by answering your prospect's unasked question, "What's in it for me?" You answer this by showing plus and/or minus benefits.

You create desire by making the prospect *want* your service or product. You do this by obtaining the prospect's confidence, through testimonials, by knowing your product and your prospect's need, by keeping your presentation simple, and through research, guarantees and company reputation.

You motivate to action by first summing up your major points. You then ask if the prospect has any questions and answer them. You then ask *your* questions, questions that fit in with your strategy to take the prospect step by step to the conclusion you want him or her to reach.

All of this works best, of course, when you *personalize* your presentation, use positive words and phrases —and avoid negative words and phrases.

The presentation is the climax of a lot of work on a salesperson's part. As Roger says, "The presentation is where it all comes together—probing, asking for the interview, researching. In football, the presentation is the Sunday afternoon game. A lot of unspectacular preparation has gone into this presentation but, once you're out there, everything is based on the game plan you agreed on beforehand. You learn about the other team while you concentrate on the basics of football. You go into the game with a good feeling about what you're going to do and what they're going to do.

"Sometimes, when you get in a game, however, you find that unusual opportunities open up. Then you have to be flexible enough to move to take advantage of those opportunities.

"In selling, it's the same way. You should know the buyer you're playing against and know his or her team. You should have a well thought-out game plan based on basic salesmanship. But, once you're in the 'game' or presentation, you've got to be able to shift with the prospect. You may have decided beforehand that this buyer needs a formal presentation and, once you're in, find that they would really prefer an informal presentation. You still follow your basic game plan, but you change the emphasis a bit to keep the buyer comfortable.

"Then, remember that only the best is good enough. Do your best each time you represent your company. Play your best each time you're on the field. The Cowboys have to know all the plays in the playbook . . . all the signals. You should know all about your product or service and a *lot* about the buyer's company. You should know more than you'll ever use; be able to answer questions frankly and accurately. Of course, if you don't know the answer, *admit* it—never try to 'fake it'—they'll know and lose respect for you."

Make each presentation your "Stradivarius" and you'll be a success!

PRESENTING REMINDERS

- Your presentation must be believed, agreed with and acted upon.
- One way to gain the prospect's attention is to dramatize the product value.

- Your presentation produces orders when it is built around buyer benefits.

- The sale is seldom closed unless your prospect has a degree of confidence in your proposition.

- Speak the prospect's language. It's a sure way to build confidence.

- In motivating the prospect to take action and give you the order, you must take the initiative.

- The important thing in getting orders is to have an established strategy you can use with confidence.

- Personalize your presentation.

- Slant your presentation to your prospect's self-interests.

- Choose impact words with motivation strength.

- You sell the product of your product.

- Be willing to let the prospect interrupt you.

- Achieve credibility. Bring on your evidence and testimonials.

- The ideal presentation uses both emotion and logic.

- Be an assistant buyer who stays in front of decision-makers with a strategy you believe in.

CHAPTER 7
STRATEGIES FOR CONTROLLING OBJECTIONS AND CONVERTING THEM INTO SALES

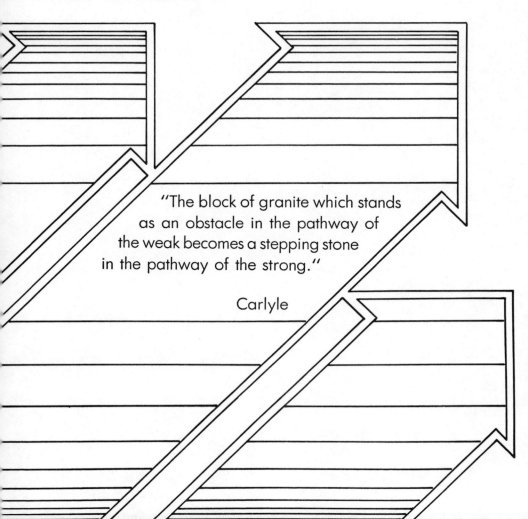

"The block of granite which stands
as an obstacle in the pathway of
the weak becomes a stepping stone
in the pathway of the strong."

Carlyle

HOW YOU STAY IN CONTROL

If you want to stay in control throughout the presentation, *write your presentation out before the appointment*. The advantage of writing out and using a standardized presentation is that it gives you complete control, no matter what your prospect says or does. Many things can and often do happen during the presentation. The prospect can interrupt. The prospect can—and generally will—interject resistances or objections. You must learn to handle these.

Your sales presentation must allow for resistances, objections and interruptions. Expect them. Prepare to meet them even before they occur. You do this by planning and writing out your presentation in advance. Knowing all that you must say and do in advance will enable you to:

- Present your facts clearly so they will be understood.
- Include the relevant points that you believe your prospect will want to know.
- Include answers to common objections you feel may be raised.
- Remember where you were in the presentation before the interruption occurred.

ALWAYS ASSERT

Study the great sales leaders in your company or in the country. They assert. These leaders are so charged with conviction that they present their conclusions as ultimate truths. They speak as individuals having authority. *Never weaken your conclusions by suggesting a doubt.* Your job is to persuade, and effective persuaders always assert. This is the principal reason they are able to overcome objections before they come up.

OUR ATTITUDE TOWARD OBJECTIONS

How should you regard objections? The inexperienced sales rep often considers an objection as a refusal to buy. To this person, an objection is viewed as a major obstacle to making the sale. *The prepared professional welcomes the objection. He or she knows it can help along the sale and not hurt it. The toughest prospect to sell isn't the one who objects but the one who shows no interest at all.* If a prospect sits in stony silence it's hard to tell where you stand. Faced with a prospect like this, you'd be praying that he or she would give you a clue. An objection is a clue to the prospect's thought processes. The antithesis of this is the prospect who *agrees* with everything you say. He or she usually doesn't buy either—because you don't know what he or she is really thinking. Again, an objection gives you a "handle," an insight.

As a skilled salesperson, objections give you the best clues to your client's reactions. Early in your sales presentation you fish for feedback to determine what the prospect's thoughts are about the points being presented. As your prospect learns more from your presentation, he or she then begins to interject objections. These objections serve as guides. Your attitude should be to welcome and expect them.

CLASSIFYING THE OBJECTION

To effectively handle an objection, you must understand what kind of objection it is. Objections fall into two general categories:

- Genuine objections
- Insincere objections

Genuine objections can be answered. Insincere objections cannot. One of the first things that will set you apart as a professional salesperson is learning to distinguish between the genuine objection and the fake.

What are the characteristics of these two kinds of objections? The insincere objection generally has the characteristic of being illogical. It is expressed through alibis, excuses or stalls. The prospect gives fictitious reasons to hide the real, genuine objection.

The genuine objection has the characteristic of truthfulness. Here the prospect feels there is a valid reason for not buying at this time. This is the easiest kind of objection to handle. In fact, it is the *only* kind of objection you *can* handle.

WHY DO PROSPECTS OBJECT?

When a prospect objects, he or she is saying, "I'm not sold . . . yet." They generally object for three reasons:

- *There is something not understood.* Your presentation has not gained understanding. You must do a better job of stating your product or service in relation to the client's need or want.

- *There is something the prospect doesn't believe.* Your presentation has not yet achieved credibility. You haven't produced enough evidence to convince the prospect of the value and owner benefits.

- *There is something the prospect is trying to cover up.* When you sense this, you must try to be considerate and build confidence.

WHEN TO ANSWER

In determining when to answer an objection, you must consider whether it is genuine or insincere and why it has surfaced. You can handle an objection before it comes up if you anticipate it. This gets easier as your experience grows. Like an actor in a long-running play, you soon not only know all of *your* lines but the lines of all of the other actors and actresses as well! Experience will teach you that there are only so many objections to your particular product or service and soon you will have heard them all. As soon as you've heard them, of course, you've also learned how to deal with them. As you've learned how to deal with them, you've learned how to anticipate them.

ANTICIPATE OBJECTIONS

Suppose, for instance, you've found a common objection to your product is that the cost is far below competition. You can anticipate that and bring out in your presentation something like, "I've had dozens of people ask me, 'How can you sell it so reasonably?' And the answer is really quite simple. Our company *invented* this process and, consequently, we've been doing it longer than anyone else. Our high volume has enabled us to retail the item for little more than other firms wholesale theirs."

IGNORE OBJECTIONS

Another way to handle an objection is to ignore it. Occasionally, you'll find it best to manage initial resistance by ignoring the response completely. In your initial contact with prospects, their resistance is likely to be high. Most people tend to react abnormally when they are in a buying situation. How many times have you noticed people shopping in a store with the idea of making a purchase? A sales clerk approaches and asks, "May I be of help?" The customer often replies, "No, I'm just looking." Generally, customers do not mean that at all. It's just a vocal pause, a defense mechanism. What they probably mean is, "I haven't lowered my resistance yet. Be patient with me. Let me learn more about what you have to offer."

In his fine book, *Meeting Objections,* Dr. J. A. Stevenson says, "The tendency to raise barriers undoubtedly originates in the same instinct which causes animals to assume a defensive attitude when brought into contact with strange objects or animals, or even familiar objects if they encroach on their domain. This resistance or defensive attitude as displayed by a prospect probably originates in the same instinct which causes a dog to bark if a stranger approaches what he considers his territory. The dog may have no real antipathy for the stranger, or the prospect any actual objection to the proposal. They both raise a sort of a barrier, however, because they are afraid of the disturbance which this unfamiliar idea or strange person may cause."

The "I don't want it/I don't need it/I can't afford it!" which so often greet you are, in reality, more often mere "barks" on the part of the prospect. "Barks," as the old saying goes, "are often worse than their bites."

ASK PERMISSION TO ANSWER THE OBJECTION LATER

One of the strategies successful salespeople have used for years in managing objections is merely to delay them. The strategy is that if you can delay a resistance, you can rob it of some of its strength. You may handle it permanently simply by delaying it. The prospect may become so wrapped up in what you say about your product or service that he or she will forget the resistance. He or she may never mention it again.

ANSWER THE OBJECTION NOW

If you feel the objection is genuine and would hinder the sale if not given a satisfactory answer, you should meet it when the prospect brings it up. To hesitate or evade may cause the objection to magnify in the prospect's mind and block the sale.

MASTER THE SIX-STEP STRATEGY

You must master a definite strategy for handling objections. You must develop an ability to react naturally, with a maximum of poise and effectiveness, whenever an objection appears to block your path.

This ability is one of the critical keys to your selling success. The sense of personal selling power derived from the confidence of having a strategy for handling objections is an invaluable asset.

These six steps should be learned and instinctively followed in any sales situation where there is an objection:

1. Hear it out.
2. Ask the prospect to repeat it.
3. Restate.
4. Isolate.
5. Use an example or story.
6. Stimulate action.

HEARING THE PROSPECT OUT

Don't evade or resent the objection. Never interrupt. Be glad it is being voiced; it shows someone is listening! It shows you've a bit more selling to do before you close, and it shows you in what area that selling must lie.

An automobile tire will gradually go flat once it has a puncture. *In somewhat the same way, your prospect's objection is likely to deflate itself once it is expressed.* When he or she gets it off his or her mind, it loses much of its steam. Listening is the basis for handling objections. How you listen is important. Lean forward. Let your facial expression register an "I'm taking your objection seriously" look.

> ### *"Let them complete your sentences, but never complete theirs."*

ASKING THE PROSPECT TO REPEAT

Take the objection seriously. Treat it with respect. *Return the ball to the prospect's court.* Often, when you ask the prospects to repeat, they will answer their own objection, or will define it in such a way that it is easier for you to handle.

RESTATING

This says to the prospect that you are listening and have understood what was said. It makes it clear you do not accept the objection as being final. Then, too, it gives you more time to think out your answer.

This restating step puts you in step with your prospect. It takes him or her off the defensive. It can help you avoid an argument. Remember, there is probably more inclination on your part to indulge in arguments when answering questions or objections than in any other part of the interview.

Few prospects are ever really convinced by argument. The members of college debating teams are always of the same conviction following the debate as they were before the debate. The members of the losing team did not have their opinions changed by the superior arguments of their opponents. In the televised presidential candidate debates (between Kennedy and Nixon, Ford and Carter, Carter and Reagan) none of the debaters switched to the opposing view as a result of the other's rhetoric.

Dr. George W. Crane, the essayist, believes that argument is poor sales strategy. He says, "Don't argue. Suggest. An ounce of suggestion is worth a ton of argument. When you suggest, it means that you get me to arrive at my own conclusion. When you argue, it means that you force me to arrive at yours. And what you want to do is to make your conclusion mine and lead me to it.

"Guide me deftly to the decision you wish me to make. Don't shove. Let my mind amble along at its own gait. I have known few men to be convinced by argument. And no women!"

The familiar philosophy, "A person convinced against his or her will is of the same opinion still," reiterates the necessity of staying on the prospect's side. We once saw a poster that said simply, "You have not converted a man simply because you have silenced him."

Let's assume that you're a sales rep for a large, well-known company and the prospect raises an objection such as, "Yes, but I'm concerned about service *after* the sale!"

You lean forward, drink it all in and restate the question. "Let me see if I understand you, Ms. Jones—you're concerned about our service *after* the sale, is that correct?" She nods and you say, "I can understand your concern, but I'm sure you'll agree that it's our *service* as much as our *products* that have made us the giant company we are today! I can assure you that service will *never* be a problem—our service department is available night and day . . ."

ISOLATING THE OBJECTION

There are always two reasons a prospect has for not deciding upon your proposition: the one that sounds good and the real reason, the genuine reason and the insincere reason. You must "smoke out" the real reason!

You do that by asking, "In addition to that, what *other* reasons do you have for not acting on this proposition today?" You must uncover the *real* reason to progress.

As you learned in the word list earlier, one of the strongest words in the English language is that little three letter word "WHY?" This powerful word can help you isolate the *real* objection. It also helps you to stay out of arguments.

For example, when your prospect says, "I can't afford it right now," restate the question and ask, "Would you mind telling me why?" The real or hidden objection will often surface.

"Locate any real obstacle and re-move it."

USING AN EXAMPLE OR STORY

More objections are overcome by emotional responses than through intellectual appeals. You can educate prospects in the soundness of your proposition, you may get them nodding vertically at every point— but unless you stir them emotionally, there is no action. Almost every student of behavior will assure you that most of us engaged in selling have too much reverence for facts. We should equip ourselves better with fresh, relevant examples and stories.

The purpose of an example or story is to help the prospect see himself or herself in the light of another person's experience. Its success lies in the fact that each of us is imitative. We will follow if relevant examples are held up in front of our eyes.

Jesus taught with parables so that people might see themselves more clearly. Lincoln used this example to explain how he felt when Douglas defeated him in the Illinois senatorial contest: "I feel like the boy who stubbed his toe. He was too big to cry and it hurt too darned much to laugh."

Carefully chosen examples and stories exert a tremendous power over the mind of the prospect.

Develop the skill of choosing and telling yours well.

STIMULATING ACTION

The only reason for answering an objection is to make the sale. The first five steps, if done properly, have moved your prospect into a position where it is more reasonable for him or her to say "yes" than to say "no."

The most important factor in stimulating action is your attitude. Always assume your prospect is going to buy now. Proceed as if all you must do is settle the few questions of minor detail.

Your attitude makes closing the sale easy and natural.

Don't be objectionable. This is not the first time the importance of avoiding arguments has been mentioned. Remove the objection without being objectionable. This is not always an easy thing to accomplish, especially when your prospect clings to an objection.

Wendell White, in his book *The Psychology of Dealing with People,* treats this subject well:

"The removal of objectionable ideas is a very delicate procedure. It can entail the danger of wounding the individual's pride. The slightest injury to another's self-esteem may become an insurmountable barrier to dissuading him or her from a committed position. To succeed in getting a person to give up an idea you must proceed in a manner that will safeguard the person's pride. There are several ways in which you can disparage an idea expressed by another person without offending."

White then offers these resistance chasers:

1. To exonerate the prospect from any blame for expressing an objection:

- "I see I have not made that point clear" or "You may feel differently with this added information."

2. To make a concession before taking exception:

- "Under normal conditions you would be correct but . . ." or "Your suggestion has much to recommend it. On the other hand . . ."

3. To reveal a deliberate attitude:

- "This is really worth considering" or "Perhaps you should secure an opinion from another before making a final decision."

Getting into arguments with prospects is one of the easiest things you can do and one of the most disastrous. There is generally a tactful, diplomatic way to remove the objection without being objectionable. Your job is to always find and employ it.

YOU DON'T HANDLE EVERY OBJECTION

The prospects you deal with have their own viewpoints, desires and prejudices. They won't respond favorably every time to what you want them to do.

Prospects will follow your advice willingly on those things that happen to be in accord with their own desires. However, they must be directed, assisted and persuaded to get the action and cooperation you desire.

There is just no sure-fire strategy for handling all prospects' objections, all of the time. There are far too many variables in each selling situation to ever formulate a guaranteed answer to all objections.

Some people who seemingly should buy, simply will not be a prospect for you. Moreover, you will find some prospects who will buy in spite of having objections. Why? They discover a reason for buying that exerts more pressure and influence than any of the negative reasons.

When the prospect really *wants* a product or service, logic goes out the window and emotion takes charge. This is human nature. Someone once observed, "People would rather have one good, solid and honest emotion in making up their minds than a thousand facts." Their motivation may be *said* to be facts when it is the emotional appeal that really lures them. This causes good salespeople to stress buyer benefits and, especially, buyer motives.

"Be an assistant buyer."

FUNCTION AS AN ASSISTANT BUYER

Throughout the book we've said, "Function as an assistant buyer." We can't say it often enough or stress it too strongly. Today's prospects are more sophisticated and informed than ever before. They consider themselves to be very knowledgeable.

By the same token, product lines are far more complex and services far more sophisticated than ever before. The most knowledgeable prospect cannot expect to stay abreast of all the changes. There is too much to know about the products and service he or she must buy.

These prospects look to you for information and guidance. Today, they are much more sensitive to the insincere and poorly informed salesperson or anything that "smacks" of manipulation. Today, prospects see through the old high-pressure techniques and gimmicks. When anything resembling high-pressure techniques, gimmicks or insincerity is detected, they immediately become suspicious. They become defensive. Their buying resistance shoots upward!

The moral is this: Stay on the prospect's side. Help him or her remove and overcome the real obstacles. This kind of attitude is essential if you are to develop an effective procedure for handling objections.

As Betty Potts of Louisville says, "The basis of every sale I make is the absolute belief on my part that my client needs my product and will profit by deciding to buy it now."

HANDLING OBJECTIONS
SUMMED UP

To handle objections, you have to stay in control. You stay in control by writing out your presentation ahead of time and by memorizing it so that you can give it naturally.

Writing out all you must say enables you to present your facts so that they will be understood, to include relevant points, to include answers to common objections and to remember where you are when interruptions or objections come.

When objections come, you'll have confidence because you're prepared. Because you're prepared, you'll *welcome* objections—they show that your prospect is still alive and listening. The first thing you want to do is classify an objection. Is it genuine or insincere? *You can only do something about genuine objections—insincere objections are hopeless.*

Prospects object because there's something they don't understand or believe, or because they're trying to cover up something.

You can deal with objections by anticipating them, ignoring them, asking permission to handle them later or by answering them now. Which strategy *you* use depends on your overall game plan and the nature of the objection.

To master objections, master six steps: Hear it out, ask that it be repeated, restate it, isolate it, use an example or story, and then stimulate action. Once the objections are out of the way, there's no reason why you shouldn't move swiftly toward the close.

You'll know where you are at all times, thanks to having taken the time to write out your presentation.

Because you have confidence, you view objections as "opposing blockers" who are trying to block your winning pass play—because to win the sale, you must pass over all these opposing objections.

In the 1979 thriller between Dallas and Washington, the Cowboys were "up." They knew their game plan, they knew their opponent, and they felt they knew what obstacles would be put in their way. They exuded confidence. They were prepared. They were ready.

As Roger puts it, "There are occasions when you might luck out and win when you're not prepared—but that's rare. Confidence doesn't count unless it's based on solid preparation."

In spite of this confidence, Dallas fell behind 17-0. But they still had confidence that they could come back. Then they went ahead 21 to 17. Then Washington bounced back and Dallas trailed 34 to 21!

Only a little over three minutes were left to go and it looked like the Cowboys were dead ducks—even some avid Dallas fans began filing out of the stadium, thinking the game was over. Dallas needed two touchdowns in three minutes!

Roger and the entire team had confidence—confidence based on preparation and an honest assessment of their ability. There were 11 objections to their making two touchdowns on the opposing team—but they were prepared to overcome those objections and win.

Dallas *did* come back and Dallas *did* win with the final score at Dallas 35, Washington 34. It went down in the books as one of the best regular season games in the 1970s.

But the game wasn't won *just* on the field, or *just* in practice, or *just* in making up the game plan. The game was won in the *minds* of each of the Dallas Cowboys and the coaching staff!

Roger had all the basic ingredients for success—he watched for the right opportunities and moved over the objections to win.

Roger has done the same in real estate. One time, he put hours into preparing what he felt was a dynamite presentation for a group of investors for an apartment complex in Tyler, Texas. He had done his homework. He had assembled potential buyers. He had put together a program that he felt would appeal to these buyers because he had prequalified them as people who needed a moderate cash flow and an extensive tax write-off.

He went in with a good game plan and played the game according to the plan. The game ended with no score.

Later that same day, Roger met another individual and, in talking with him, realized that he too met the investor profile. Using the same game plan, he went on to close the sale—and that one man purchased the entire complex!

Was Roger discouraged when he lost the first game? Certainly he was disappointed, but Roger has taught himself to be a percentage player, just as we all have to be. He knew that there was nothing wrong with the product and nothing wrong with the presentation. He was willing to continue to play the game until he scored—and he did.

He overcame objections and proceeded until the game opened up and he had an eligible receiver down field—and won.

HANDLING OBJECTIONS
REMINDERS

- You stay in control in selling by having a planned presentation.
- Sales leaders speak as individuals having authority.
- Objections offer important clues. Welcome them.
- Objections are either insincere or genuine.
- Prospects raise objections when they don't understand, don't believe or are trying to cover up.
- Common objections can be anticipated. Handle them before they come up.
- Objections can be ignored or they can be deferred.
- Asking the prospect to repeat an objection shows your sincerity.
- Restating the objection shows you are listening and gives you an opportunity to think.
- Isolating the objection smokes out the real reason.
- More objections are overcome through emotional responses than through intellectual appeals.
- The most important factor in stimulating action is having confidence in a strategy.
- Don't argue. Handle objections without being objectionable.
- When the prospect really wants a product or service, logic slips away.
- Prospects look to you for information and guidance.

CHAPTER 8

LEADING THE PROSPECT TO THE BUYING DECISION

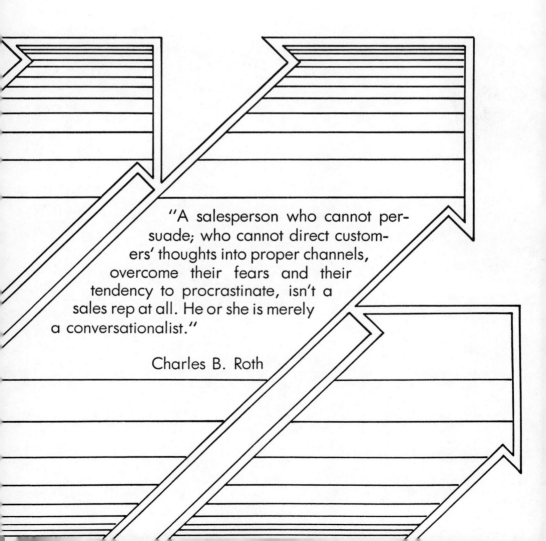

"A salesperson who cannot persuade; who cannot direct customers' thoughts into proper channels, overcome their fears and their tendency to procrastinate, isn't a sales rep at all. He or she is merely a conversationalist."

Charles B. Roth

AN EFFECTIVE SALESPERSON CLOSES

An effective salesperson closes, and a poor closer is *always* an ineffective salesperson. *The close is the main event which the entire selling process aims toward.*

"The entire selling process is a closing process."

Everything that has gone before—planning, prospecting, making contact, probing, presenting, handling objections and all of the other activity and effort—has been focused on this main objective. The sales rep who cannot close is like the football team that rolls up impressive yardage but lacks the punch to move the ball across the goal line.

You may hear someone described as "a pretty good salesperson but not a strong closer." Since closing does require strategy, there may be some truth in this analysis. However, the problem generally lies throughout the selling process. The sales rep who is

157

strong all the way through the selling process will not ordinarily become weak at completing the sale.

Drive into your mind this truth: The entire selling process is a closing process. Closing, when properly done, is a natural and rather obvious experience.

FIVE CARDINAL RULES OF SELLING TO REMEMBER

Every person has a personality that is different from all others. We see successful sales reps who are bold and aggressive. They have little difficulty asking prospects for anything. We see effective salespeople who are sensitive and somewhat quiet. They have to muster courage every time they ask for an order.

Regardless of what type of personality you have, you can become a stronger closer. You can turn the toughest prospect into a willing buyer, ready and eager to do business with *you—if* you regularly use these five cardinal rules of selling:

1. *If you would win a prospect to your cause, first convince him or her that you are a genuine friend.*

2. *Help the prospect recognize a need.* Uncover the basic need and stick with it.

3. *Keep in mind the prospect is best convinced by reasons he or she discovers.* There is only one way to get anybody to do anything; that is, by making the other person want to do it.

4. *Always plan to demonstrate the value and benefit your product or service provides.*

5. *Make it easy for the prospect to buy from you.* You do this by getting your prospect into the position where it is more reasonable to say "yes" than "no."

DEAL WITH DECISION-MAKERS

As a professional salesperson your time is valuable. Make certain you don't waste it by telling your story "for the practice" to someone who can't make a buying decision.

Frank Calari, Sr., of Los Angeles has consistently ranked at the top of his company's production honor role. Frank feels that you'll improve your closing ratio by as much as 100 percent if you're firm in your resolve to only make a presentation where a decision-maker is present! Frank says this is especially important in dealing with husband-wife situations or partnerships. "Their response is altogether different when they are alone, and this weakens your position. If you don't have both together, wait until you can!"

THE TWO VITAL CLOSING FACTORS

The most important factor in closing is not your proposition, your price or business conditions. The most important factor is *you.*

Since you must do the closing, *your mental attitude and your method are more important than anything else.* To be a successful closer, you must develop a closing consciousness—and then, you must have a closing strategy.

Closing Consciousness

This is an attitude of expectancy. It is your absolute belief that you will close the business. This feeling will perform for you. It will be transferred to your prospect naturally, without conscious effort. Your prospect will begin to feel as you do. He or she will expect to buy.

"The most useful sales tool I have ever found is *imagining a desired outcome,*" says Joe McKinney. This has proved consistently reliable for Joe, a former securities broker and investment banker who is now the chief executive officer for Tyler Corporation.

Joe says, "Visualize the outcome in Technicolor, three dimensions and high fidelity. See yourself executing a document, writing the order and shaking hands with a sold prospect. Do it with as much vivid detail as your imagination can develop. *Feel the pressure of the handshake and experience the elation that engulfs your entire being as you receive the expected news that you have the order.*"

Steve Stone became the top winning pitcher in Baltimore Oriole baseball history. In the process he won the coveted Cy Young Award. Steve was asked how he made such a dramatic change in his performance. Like Joe McKinney, Steve credited his remarkable success to *"the mental practice I have on the day I am pitching."*

Steve says, "I see myself pitching masterfully to each hitter. I am using the pitches they can't hit. I sense the scene which follows the final out—the roar of the crowd—the congratulations of my teammates and manager. I see myself reading the morning newspaper account of my victory. I capture the winning feeling all the way."

This winning feeling never makes itself known in so many words. You never insult your prospects by implying you know their needs better than they do. Your expectancy works through your manner and actions. It is always there—in your expressions, your responses, the way in which you handle the order blank, in the ways in which you demonstrate or explain your product or service. You expect the prospect to buy now. *You engender qualities in the prospect's mind like those you display.*

> *"Believe in your product,*
> *believe in yourself—*
> *belief produces behavior."*

Closing consciousness takes planning and finesse. It pays off in sales.

Closing Strategy

You must learn to create your own closing opportunities. Most of the sales you make will not close themselves. You must guide and direct the prospect's behavior. Here again, you play the role of an assistant buyer.

Let's say your prospect has been attentive but indicated no strong interest to move forward. There has been no nodding of the head, no handling of the product, no asking of particularly revealing questions. It is a common error for you to assume that because no interest has been expressed, none exists. In most cases, you must do more than watch passively for indications of interest. You must create the situation in which interest can reveal itself.

We recommend you adopt a four-step strategy for closing:

- Summarize.
- Ask for your prospect's questions.
- Ask your questions.
- Stimulate action.

Summarize. Emphasize the buyer benefits. Benefits and features are blended together in such a manner that your summation accomplishes its purpose of refreshing the prospect's memory. In this step you assure by affirmation and create understanding by repetition.

Ask for Your Prospect's Questions. You are probing for any major objections. You don't ask for objections; it wouldn't sound right. Instead, you ask for questions. The end result is the same—it smokes out any objections.

"Questions uncover closing opportunities."

Ask Your Questions. Take the prospect's mind off the big decision and put it on the little ones. Obviously, the big decision in every sale is, "Will you buy now?" Develop a series of little questions you can ask that gain agreement on minor points. If your prospect is not quite ready to buy, your questions will merely seem a part of your normal routine. If the prospect is ready to buy, he or she will cooperate by answering your questions easily and naturally. Develop the feeling that it is the prospect's decision to move forward. You strengthen the close in this step by recording on the order blank the prospect's responses.

Stimulate Action. This final step is one shared by all the effective closers we have ever observed. You must start to do something that the prospect must stop you from doing if he or she wants to avoid giving an order. You must follow through to the end.

Getting your prospect's approval and signature is the logical conclusion. The confident manner in which you proceed to gain action provides leadership for the prospect. Your strongest weapon in combating reluctance and fear is your manner in this step. More than ever you must be sure you are confident, self-assured and poised.

"Make it more reasonable for the prospect to say 'yes' than 'no.' "

GAUGE THE PROSPECT'S PACE

Every person has his or her own pace. Your ability to gauge it can be an important asset.

Judging a prospect's pace is not all that difficult when you understand its importance. Study each prospect closely. Does he or she comprehend your presentation quickly? Does his or her mind seem to "jump" to conclusions? If so, he or she will probably make the decisions to buy in the same way. On the other hand, if the prospect seems to hesitate, if he or she pauses, asks many questions, and mulls over the answers, the chances are you're dealing with a slow, methodical buyer. He or she will be a deliberate decision-maker.

It is important to form an estimate of each prospect's rate of thinking because you must follow his or her pace to make the most sales. If the prospect is always thinking ahead of your presentation, he or she is going to become impatient. If you move too quickly, the prospect is going to feel he or she is being rushed. In either case, you will not be effective.

You must walk at the prospect's pace if you're going to guide him or her to your destination—a sale.

"Sell at the prospect's pace."

A LANGUAGE YOU MUST LEARN

Every creature sends out signals about its feelings and attitudes. The cat purrs when contented and arches its back when angry. The dog growls when angry and wags its tail when it wants to be friendly. The baby signals wants by laughing or crying.

These reactions are caused by certain pressures within the mind and body, which respond almost automatically to given situations. In selling we refer to similar reactions on the part of prospects as "buying signs."

You will improve your selling effectiveness by studying the response reactions of prospects. Theirs is a language you will need to master. Learn to observe the common signals prospects flash that can be valuable progress reports.

Knowing how to read the buying signs of prospects provides you with a competitive edge. Nearly every buyer will show some signal when he or she is ready or almost ready to make a decision.

WHEN TO STOP SELLING

Much has been written about the "psychological moment" to make the close. Today most students of selling believe that "the moment" can be created several times throughout the selling process. They advocate to close early, to close late . . . to close anytime the prospect gives you the indication that he or she is ready to buy.

In the typical sale, there probably is a rising interest level that turns to desire. *By staying alert, you can learn to "feel" the prospect's attitude.* Although you may not be able to describe precisely how you know, you will feel it through a sort of sixth sense.

BUYING SIGNS TO WATCH FOR

Learn to watch for these indications:

- **Words and Questions.** These are some of the most important buying signs. What your prospect says and how he or she says it can be very meaningful. Questions should almost always be interpreted as buying signs. Some examples include, "What discount do you allow for cash?" or "How long would it take for delivery?" Questions of any kind indicate interest. Questions as pointed as these tell you your prospect is waiting for you to bring the interview to a close.

- **Prospect's Attention.** The prospect's attitude often betrays his or her interest. The prospect leans forward, rubs his or her chin, pulls an ear or scratches his or her head. These actions are revealing an "almost persuaded" attitude. Likewise, when a prospect reexamines the product or contract, the time has arrived for you to close.

- **An Act of Hesitation.** When your prospect hesitates just for a moment over one article or item, this is an important signal.

- **Tone of Voice.** Even a slight raising or lowering of the tone of voice will give you an indication of interest.

- **Facial Expressions.** Most people betray their thinking in their expressions. Watch your prospect's eyes for a look of interest. Many feel that eyes tell you more than words.

Emulate the successful pros in selling. Stay alert—pay

attention. Be able to recognize and read your prospects through the body language and other indicators we have described. Whenever you are reasonably sure of your "feel," then act—attempt a close.

SEVEN AND ONE-HALF STRATEGIES FOR CLOSING THE SALE

There are at least seven and one-half strategies for closing the sale. The selection of the particular strategy for a certain situation is up to you. It depends on the type of prospect you are selling, the timing, your judgment and your selling style.

What we are giving you now are the basic strategies. Become thoroughly familiar with each of them. Then, put your imagination to work. You will create many variations that will make these strategies even more effective.

1. **Closing by Assuming.** When you use this strategy, you are taking it for granted your prospect will buy. *Let the prospect see and feel your undoubting attitude about his or her buying from you now.*

2. **Closing on a Minor Point.** It is easier for anyone to make a minor decision than a major one. Using this strategy, you make it easier for the prospect by avoiding the major decision.

   You use this strategy whenever there is a choice between two appeals. The choice is given to the prospect. It might be a simple question like, "Would your investment be registered as an individual or as tenants in common?" or "Should we ask our legal department to prepare the contract papers or will your lawyers draw them up?" or "Would you prefer white or blue?" or "Would you prefer to have someone pick them up or have us deliver?"

Take the prospect's mind off the big decisions and put it on the little ones. You will make more sales.

"Make it easy for the prospect to buy."

3. **Impending Event.** Psychologists tell us the fear of loss is an especially strong motivating force. Using this strategy, you tell your prospect of some impending event that necessitates immediate action if the prospect is to avoid losing something of value.

   People usually want what is difficult to get. It is contrary to human nature to let an opportunity slip. It is an inborn trait.

   This "last chance" strategy is a favorite of life insurance agents. For years, they have closed many sales because of an impending age change. Real estate brokers remind prospects, "At this price, this property won't last long." Salespeople remind prospects that products will be more expensive in the future or that the "sale ends Saturday."

   The prospect is made to feel that he or she must buy *now* to avoid a loss.

   Use this strategy to rout procrastination. You'll find it is one of the best weapons in your closing arsenal, *if* you're honest. Don't tell a prospect, "This offer is good only if you buy *now*—I can't make it tomorrow." It's usually not true and almost never believable.

4. **Closing with Physical Action.** It pays to *do* something as well as *say* something when attempting to

close. *Action is a most persuasive language.* Many times action without words will serve the same purpose, such as clearing a space to fill out the order blank, getting your pen ready to use or just pulling a chair closer to the desk.

The principle of this strategy is this: *Start to do something the prospect will have to stop you from doing if he or she wants to avoid giving an order.* You are sure to discover that most prospects will permit you to go ahead and write up the order. They will then proceed to sign it rather than interrupt the progress of your leadership action. This is a strategy used by almost all strong closers. It produces orders.

5. **Closing with Emotion.** Emotion and impulse influence more people to action than do reason or logic. Most strong closers are master storytellers. They find a story to be a useful motivational tool. It brings a third-party endorsement into play which often becomes the turning point of an interview.

For example, the pro at your country club talks with you about a new set of irons. You feel your present set is good enough. The timing isn't right—you have a tax bill to pay. Logically, the new clubs must wait. But then, the pro tells you about Danny Reeves. He purchased the same irons last month and has taken three strokes off his score. This emotional appeal moves you into action. Impulse now overcomes reason.

Equip yourself with interesting stories and examples that appeal to pride, fear and self-esteem. Your prospect will identify with the hero in your story. The prospect sees, point by point, the parallel between your story and his or her own. Emotion wins—plain common sense doesn't have a chance!

The stories you tell must be told well. No matter how busy or distracted the prospect might be, you want to capture his or her attention. Telling stories is an art. Like any other art, you have to practice and work at it to get it perfect.

Examine the stories told by the next really good public speaker you hear. Listen to the stories of professional humorists like Jerry Clower. It isn't the stories *themselves* that are so funny—it's the exciting, dramatic way that they're *told*. Learn some sales stories that illustrate your points. Then learn to tell them well.

6. **Closing by Inducement.** One of the chief enemies to closing sales is procrastination. This strategy recognizes that procrastination operates against you most of the time. An inducement enables you to close in spite of it.

   This sales inducer rests its case on one of the most fundamental of human appeals—the desire to get something for nothing. "During the month of January, we will install your antenna without charge" or "If you can agree to the lease arrangement during June, you will be given free rent until October."

   Your success in using the inducement strategy will depend on *how* you use it. It can be viewed as a high-pressure tactic. Used properly and tactfully, it constitutes an effective closing aid.

   Along this line, form the habit of offering related items. Selling related items and/or selling special low-priced goods is a strategy used by most high-performing sales reps. This helps you sell more than the customer intended to buy. It boosts your average sale and it often gains a new customer for you. Jayne Kinder sells for Xerox. She doesn't stop with just selling equipment. *She keeps probing until she finds a related need.* If she can't sell a copier, she sells ribbons or computer forms. Her new customer receives direct mail catalogs and other Xerox supply incentives. "Now that these prospects have bought something from me," Jayne says, "it will make selling them a copier that much easier." Use it as a closing strategy— any sale is better than no sale.

7. **Closing by Asking Them to Buy.** One way to get an order is to ask for it. Purchasing agents and buyers say that it is amazing how many sales reps seem unable to bring themselves to ask for the order.

We're reminded of the life insurance agent who was a close personal friend of Henry Ford. The agent read of Ford's purchase of a substantial policy from another agent. He stormed in to see Mr. Ford and exploded, "Why in h--- didn't you buy the policy from me?" Henry Ford's reply was reported to have been, "Why in h--- didn't you *ask* me?"

Sometimes it is smart to forget the complex strategies and simply ask for the business boldly and frankly.

7½. **Closing with Silence.** A most powerful influence in controlling others is silence. Nature abhors a vacuum and silences must be filled. Many times, an effective close puts the prospect into the role of being the salesperson. In other words, the prospects feel they should *sell* you on why they *don't* need your product or service.

The toughest person in the world to sell is one who doesn't talk. Now you be that person who doesn't talk! Use silence. The prospect will become unpoised. Few can stand silence. Often, buying signs will surface at this precise time.

Silence requires courage on your part. Practice until you can use it without difficulty. You will discover you can control the buyer with your silence as effectively as you can control him or her with your words. Silence will help you do much to "smoke out" buying signs and close sales.

Silence can be golden.

ASSIST THE BUYER WITH THESE QUESTIONS

Lynn Newman, a fine graphic sales rep, believes there are five important questions the prospect must answer before deciding to buy. We agree with Lynn. Here are Lynn's five vital questions:

- Do I need the owner benefit this product provides?
- Is this the single best answer to my need?
- Is this the right source?
- Is the price right?
- When should I buy?

Whatever your product or service, think of your prospect as having to make these five decisions before giving you the order. Then do your best to assist your buyer in making all of them affirmative.

This practice will strengthen your effectiveness and improve your closing ratio.

ASK YOURSELF THESE QUESTIONS

If you are not closing a favorable percentage of your interviews, refer to this check-up on closing effectiveness. Reviewing these questions regularly will improve your closing ratio:

- Did I make it easier for my prospect to say "yes" than "no"?
- Did I display poise and enthusiasm which showed in my words and actions?
- Was my speed of delivery too slow? The average sales rep talks much too slowly. Most talk at a rate of 135 words per minute. The average prospect thinks at a rate of 1,500 words per minute. Don't let the prospect's mind wander by talking too slowly.
- Did I wear my prospect out with too many facts? Were there too few examples and picture elements in the presentation?
- Were my statements vague and unclear?
- Did I do my homework to enable me to answer questions intelligently?
- Did I focus on buyer benefits?
- Did I embrace the ABC principle—*Always Be Closing?*
- Did I listen effectively?
- Did I prepare my summary?
- Did I make it too hard for the prospect to buy?
- Did I ask the prospect to buy enough times?

It's been our experience that a failure to close seldom leads to a sale later on. As Roger says, "When you leave a prospect saying, 'I'll think it over and call you,' don't expect a phone call. It's rare that someone decides to buy later. Usually, if it's a good prospect and you've done your homework and presented it properly and made a strong close, you'll leave the office having made a sale."

CLOSING SUMMED UP

Next to the first four minutes, the most important part of your sales interview is the time when you close the sale.

In a well-planned sales presentation, there should always be several such closing moments. Remember the ABC's of selling—*A*lways *B*e *C*losing!

Each time you drive home one of the important selling points in favor of your proposition, ask for the order. Attempt to close then. If you're unsuccessful, stay with your presentation, driving home the buyer benefits.

You are somewhat like the football team that tries one offensive play after another until it discovers what tactic will score and win.

No one buys anything unless he or she feels that it is in his or her interest. This is why your summary talk is so important. It must convince the prospect of the ways in which your product or service will benefit him or her.

Prepare to make it much more reasonable for the prospect to say "yes" than "no" to what you are selling.

In closing, nothing is more contagious than enthusiasm. Effective sales reps are excited about what they have to sell. Radiate confidence, goodwill and genuine sincerity in what you say and the way you say it.

Finally, remember that the way to close is through your dominant attitude of expectancy coupled with planned strategy. It is *impossible* to close too soon. It is entirely *possible* to close too late! The time to close is whenever it can be done effectively; and the sooner the better!

CLOSING REMINDERS

- The entire selling process is a closing process.
- To win a prospect to your cause, first convince him or her you are a friend.
- Always demonstrate value and benefit.
- Make it easy for the prospect to buy from you.
- An important closing factor is closing consciousness.
- Make it more reasonable for the prospect to say "yes."
- Questions uncover selling opportunities.
- Sell at the prospect's pace.
- Decide that you must stimulate the closing action.
- Learn to read the language that has to do with buying signs.
- When you "take it for granted" you are closing by assuming.
- Put the prospect's mind on little decisions.
- The fear of loss is a powerful motivator.
- Emotion influences more people to action than does logic.
- A chief enemy of closing is procrastination.
- Using silence to close sales requires a courageous attitude.
- A sales rep's job is to sell, and selling means closing sales that don't close themselves.

CHAPTER 9

REMEMBERING SERVICE AND FOLLOW-THROUGH AFTER THE SALE

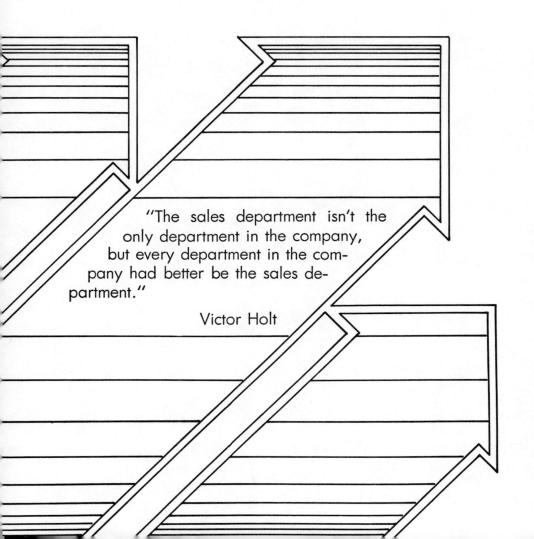

"The sales department isn't the only department in the company, but every department in the company had better be the sales department."

Victor Holt

THE IMPORTANCE OF
FOLLOW-THROUGH

The salesperson who stops selling when he or she has the order is destined to stay among the ranks of the mediocre. Your work is by no means ended when you leave after a successful selling effort. *Today, more and more customers are coming to appreciate service and follow-through as a thing of value in making buying decisions.*

More and more companies are emphasizing service not only as a means of keeping satisfied customers but as an added "initial sales value." Life insurance agents are now offering a ten-day free look. Automobile salespeople are stressing longer warranty periods. This same sales psychology is spreading to other fields as well.

If your product will last longer and require fewer repairs, if it is covered by a longer or better warranty, or if your capacity for service is greater or more convenient—point out these values to the prospect. *A reputation for prompt, courteous and reliable service often means more to a buyer than does the price of the product being sold.*

Building customer satisfaction in today's business climate is more and more the result of the personal service you promise and deliver after the sale is made. Customer satisfaction is essential to good business. Make customer satisfaction your "stock in trade."

"There is one thing you can always give which makes your product unique—a better buy than your prospect can hope to find elsewhere." Joe Johnson of Georgetown, Kentucky, said that and he adds, "That one additional ingredient is your personal service." Joe tells his many customers, "Stop for service where service never stops."

We talked to Jerry Griffin, the nation's leading Cadillac salesman four times in the past six years. Jerry's entire approach centers on building a lasting relationship. Jerry tells the prospect, "I want to help you get what you want. I'm not interested in selling a car, I'm interested in building a customer. I want all the cars you buy in the future." We discovered that Jerry ties his buyers to him in many ways. For example, he employs a full-time assistant to provide free delivery service whenever the buyer needs his or her automobile serviced!

Randy Heady, a top real estate salesman, sums it up well when he says, "Quick commissions I don't need—lasting clients I do!"

SHOW THEM YOUR APPRECIATION

All of your customers have one thing in common—each one is hungry for sincere appreciation. Most feel that others do not recognize or appreciate their true worth. Praise and appreciation can work wonders in building long-lasting, viable relationships.

Consider how *you* feel when someone shows you sincere appreciation. Sincere appreciation gives you a lift. It makes your whole day brighter. You develop a feeling of kinship and liking for the person who takes the time to appreciate you. You must create these same feelings in your customers. You might ask, "Why don't more people use this technique?" This is a question that has no logical answer. Properly used, praise and appreciation are strong factors in building and maintaining relationships.

"What can I do to favorably stand out in my customer's mind?"

If you want to become an effective relationship builder, start looking for ways in which you can show genuine appreciation. You have, of course, some natural times when you should always show your appreciation:

1. **Express your appreciation for each order received.** Appreciation for new orders is usually automatic. The following is an example of the kind of expression we recommend:

> Mr. Robert S. Schoder
> 1516 Woodward Avenue
> Detroit, Michigan 75603
>
> Dear Bob:
>
> Just a note to say "thank you" and let Val and you know that we appreciate doing business with you very much. As the years roll on, I assure you that both my company and I will strive to merit your confidence.

Since changes in family and financial conditions make it desirable to review your life insurance plan periodically, I will keep in touch with you and call on you from time to time.

Naturally, I will consider it a privilege to be consulted by you and your friends whenever the subject of life insurance comes up. Bob, I would like very much to have you consider me your life insurance man.

Sincerely yours,

Jack Murray, CLU

2. **Give appreciation to those who assist you.** It is good to give appreciation to those who assist you in any way to reach and sell your new customer. These might include receptionists, assistants, secretaries, etc. They can be most helpful to you in building a relationship.

All of us have made a habit of sending thank-you's to those who have helped us. Roger has carried it a step further and jots down the name of each secretary he talks to and keeps it right beside the boss's name. Then, the next time he calls, he can call the secretary by name. This goes a long way in getting Roger interviews. After all, isn't memorizing someone's name a way of saying, "You're important"?

Now if the boss has been busy and hard to catch, who is going to get preferential treatment—a salesperson who is on a first-name basis with the secretary or one from a competing company who's brisk and business-like?

Roger says you'd be surprised what a card or a short

thank-you to a secretary will do to your stock in a company too!

3. **Always express appreciation for an interview.** You should always give appreciation to the prospect who grants you an interview, even though he or she does not buy. This is one of the best ways to make an impression and to keep the prospect's mind open to your proposition at a future date. When the need or opportunity arises to consider a change, he or she will be inclined to remember you.

4. **Show appreciation through your manners and actions.** Your manners and actions reveal your appreciation. Let the buyer know where you can be reached whenever you are needed. This tells your customer you appreciate his or her business and want to keep it. Returning telephone calls promptly shows your appreciation, as does being an attentive listener.

5. **Look for opportunities.** Look for opportunities to recognize any special occasions or achievements. It shows your interest. Scout trade papers, local papers and the like for news of promotions or advancements. Be aware of the impending birth of a child. Then send a clipping with a short congratulatory note—it shows you care!

6. **Give thanks for referrals.** Always express appreciation to those customers who refer business to you. By all means, report back to them on your results.

7. **Send prospects to your customers.** If your customers are also in business, send them prospects or supply them with leads. This is an effective way to develop an on-going relationship. It is just natural for a person to respond favorably to you when you show your appreciation and helpfulness.

The basic principle to follow is this one: Never forget a customer and never let a customer forget you.

SERVE WHAT YOU SELL

Your customers will be presented claims and counter-claims from people who offer similar products at about the same price. The competitive edge you want to develop comes from the attitude you project of serving as you sell. You do this in two ways.

First, you do whatever it takes to establish a record of consistent reliability. Earning the reputation of being a 100 percent reliable sales rep whose every word and promise can be depended upon takes application, effort and attention to detail.

Second, you stay determined to be the best-informed sales rep who calls on your customers. This requires a commitment to excellence and a regular program of study.

Once you have established the image of being a reliable, well-informed salesperson, you are in an enviable position.

"Never forget a customer.
Never let a customer forget you."

HANDLE COMPLAINTS—FAST!

Customer satisfaction can be evaluated in most companies by studying the company's policy and record in handling complaints. When complaints are handled courteously, promptly and reliably, complaining customers are retained as customers.

Sooner or later, you are going to run into a complaining customer. The complaint may be minor or major. It may be a mistake in billing or shipping. It could be an unwarranted letter from your credit department.

Whether or not the complaint appears to be reasonable, *your objective is to handle the complaint courteously, promptly and reliably.*

There are certain rules you should follow. The first rule is to listen. Do not interrupt—wait until the customer has talked it out. Second, always thank the customer for calling the complaint to your attention. Next, carefully evaluate what action can be taken to rectify the situation. Finally, report back to the customer promptly.

During any period of adjustment, be certain you keep the customer informed. Let him or her know what action is taking place until full restitution has been made or until you have reached agreement.

Your aim is to maintain customer satisfaction if at all possible.

FIVE KEYS TO SERVING BETTER

A team of some of America's most eminent psychologists, psychiatrists, sociologists and financial experts developed five key ways to be happier, healthier and live longer.

Their remarkable recipe for the "good life" will work just as well in achieving and maintaining customer satisfaction. The golden keys are these:

1. Value your relationships.
2. Think of others and how you can help them.
3. Be positive about yourself, your business and your future.
4. Strive for stability in your personal and business life.

5. Work hard to give more than you get out of every relationship.

Make it a practice to follow this recipe. You will serve better. Your customers will feel more secure—and you'll feel better about yourself.

YOU ARE THE FIRM

Always be mindful of your aura of influence. *Professionals in selling always identify themselves with their companies.* They never say "the company," it is always "we." The customer cannot talk about your company without including you. You cannot refer to your company without including yourself. In your customer's eyes, you do more than represent the firm—you *are* the firm.

Here's a quotation we saw at the reception desk of a Dallas hotel some years ago. It describes the influence of a single individual.

An institution may spread itself over the entire business community. It may employ all kinds of people . . . but the average person will almost always form a judgment of it through contacts with *one individual*.

If this person is discourteous, inefficient or ineffective, it will take much time and energy to overcome that bad impression.

Each member of an organization who in any capacity comes in contact with the public is an agent, and the impression made is an advertisement, good or bad, which will make an indel-

ible impression on the mind of the prospect.

As Dr. Albert Schweitzer said:

"I don't know what your destiny will be but one thing I know, the only ones among you who will be really happy are those who will have sought and found how to serve."

Dr. Schweitzer could have been describing you and your career in selling. "The person profits most who sells and serves best." Be determined to deliver better service than your competition. You will profit most!

SELLING AFTER THE SALE SUMMED UP

One of your biggest and best sales tools is service. Successful salespeople soon find, as we have, that most of their business comes from either former customers or referrals from former customers. Today, more and more customers are beginning to appreciate service and follow-through—so much so that it enters into their buying decisions.

If your product has service advantages, whether it is length of life, time between recommended service or speed of service, be sure to point them out.

The world is full of similar products, similarly priced. Your product has one distinct advantage: *your service!* Your service can be the cutting edge *if* you show your clients your appreciation.

How do you show your appreciation? By thanking

them for each order received. By showing your appreciation to those who assist you. By expressing appreciation for an interview. By showing appreciation through your manners and actions. By looking for opportunities to show your appreciation. By giving thanks for referrals.

Service what you sell. Never forget a customer and never let a customer forget you. *"To give real service you must add something which cannot be bought or measured with money—sincerity and integrity,"* wrote Donald Adams. This is something that can't be faked, at least not for long. If you have the best interest of your people at heart, it will show in your actions time and time again. You'll build a reservoir of goodwill.

If you have complaints (and you eventually will!) handle them fast. Let the customer "get it off his or her chest." Learn to listen. Be courteous. Take immediate action and keep the customer advised of what is being done.

There are five keys that unlock the good life and they relate to all facets of life, including service.

They are: value your relationships; think of others and how to help them; be positive about yourself, your business and your future; strive for stability; and work hard to give more than you get.

Remember that *you are the firm.* You are the company in the minds of your customers. If you do a good job, then your company does a good job. If you perform poorly, then your company performs poorly.

We tend to judge ourselves by what we want to be—others judge us by what we are. *Be* the salesperson you want to be—learn to sell with service!

SELLING AFTER THE SALE
REMINDERS

- All of your customers have one thing in common—they are hungry for appreciation.
- Praise and appreciation are strong factors in building relationships.
- Express your appreciation for each order received.
- Give appreciation to those who assist you in making sales.
- Your manners and actions reveal your appreciation.
- The basic law, "Never forget a customer," will continue to stand and apply in any age.
- To serve as you sell, establish a record of consistent reliability.
- Be and stay an informed sales rep.
- Handle any and all complaints courteously, promptly and reliably.
- Professionals always identify themselves with their companies.

CHAPTER 10

HOW TO PROFIT FROM TIME MANAGEMENT IN SELLING

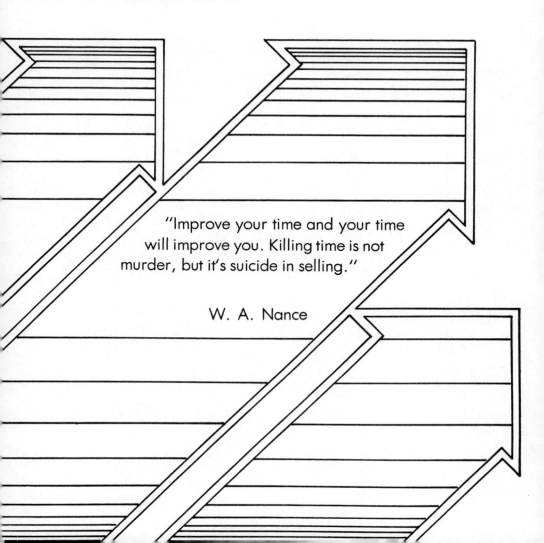

"Improve your time and your time
will improve you. Killing time is not
murder, but it's suicide in selling."

W. A. Nance

A SLIGHT IMPROVEMENT

In the Kipling Room at the Toronto Library, a plaque reads, "What you do when you don't have to determines what you will be when you can no longer help it!" Quite often those "things you do when you don't have to" will be the important things you do consciously and routinely to manage your selling time.

"Too little time," complain many salespeople today. Too much to do and not nearly enough time to get it done—too many crises, too many interruptions, too many problems, too many changes in plans. How often have you said to yourself, "If only I could add an extra hour or so to my selling day!" Normally, you can be expected to work 100,000 hours during your lifetime. Obviously, often a slight improvement in time management makes a big difference in your bottom-line production.

The urge for more time is nothing new. Napoleon, in the heat of battle, once said to an aide, "Go sir, and gallop! And remember that the world was made in six days! Ask of me anything you wish—except time!"

You *can* have more time, *if* you're willing to plan for it.

YOU CAN GIVE YOURSELF A RAISE

In sales, you are measured and rewarded not by the hours you put in but by what you put in the hours. The quality of selling time is a function of what you spend it doing, where you spend it, how you spend it, and with whom you spend it.

Here's a study we've made ourselves and encouraged many people in sales to make. You'll find it quite revealing.

First, buy or borrow a stopwatch. Be careful which kind you get. You will need the kind used to time athletic events—not the kind that resets to zero after every stop.

Second, take the watch with you every day for a week of normal selling. Keep it in your pocket. Turn it on and let it run every moment you are actually in the presence of a prospect. It goes on only when you are talking to a prospect about your products or service, in other words, *while you are selling.* Don't let the watch run while you are driving around deciding whom you will call. Don't let it run while you are "shooting the breeze," even with a prospect. Don't let it run while you wrestle through paperwork in the office or while you are having coffee. In short, don't let the watch run while you are doing anything but making an actual sales call. Next, don't tell your manager about your experiment. Your manager might ask to read the watch! Don't talk about it to your associates. You can tell them later when they start asking about your improved production records and larger commission checks. Since the stopwatch readings are for you, and *you alone,* there will be very little temptation to cheat. After all, you are trying to bolster your *income*—not your *ego.*

Finally, add up the daily readings at the end of the week. If you find (as most who make honest measurements will find) that during the whole week you spent less than ten hours of new, creative sales effort in front of your prospects, don't be discouraged.

Don't be discouraged even if the readings for the week total less than five hours! It's okay to be *shocked*—but don't be *discouraged*.

After you recover from shock, you'll realize that you have gotten to the heart of your most important problem: time. *The problem is that you aren't earning the kind of money you could easily be earning because you aren't spending enough hours making calls.* Sure, you're putting in the hours! But now you know that few of those hours are productive, selling hours. The other hours are being frittered away!

To increase your productivity and income you won't need to work any *harder*—but you will need to work *smarter*.

Working smarter means you need to spend less time on:

- paperwork during your most productive hours
- expensive cups of coffee
- pleasant but expensive conversations
- unnecessary footwork

Regardless of where those extra hours go, if you have timed your actual selling time, you know exactly what your most important problem is. It's managing your time.

Six most common time problems:

- *Unplanned meetings*
- *Lack of organization*
- *No-shows*

- *Poor scheduling of calls*
- *Procrastination*
- *"Fire-fighting"*

HIGH-QUALITY VS. LOW-QUALITY TIME

To an engineer, lawyer or accountant, time is simply a quantity, a number of seconds, minutes and hours. In the quantitative view they take, every hour is equal to every other hour. This is not so in your case. Clearly, you have high-quality time and low-quality time. One of your hours will be very productive when all other hours are wasted. An hour spent in front of a prospect may produce a very big money-making result for you. An hour spent in filing, which may be necessary, will never make you very rich. *Remember, you are paid for results—not for your hours.*

Because time management is vital to every salesperson's success, we've extensively researched the subject and studied various remedies. You'll find the time management principles developed here to be practical. You can start using them today to make maximum use of your selling time.

In our research we reached a couple of important conclusions. First, as stated above, in any type of sales work a slight improvement in time management produces a marked improvement in bottom-line results. Second, if you condense the many articles written and thoughts developed with reference to time management, you will discover that the most sound approach to sound time management revolves around mastering five principles:

1. Developing a time-conscious attitude
2. Planning your priorities daily

3. Staying effective

4. Establishing and maintaining momentum

5. Developing a sense of urgency by setting deadlines

Let's examine some specific suggestions in each of these important areas.

Developing Time-Consciousness

Like most success factors in selling, time management is largely dependent upon attitude. Shape your attitude so that you become aware of time and the manner in which you use it. Time is one of the major resources to utilize if you achieve outstanding selling success. An outstanding salesman in New Jersey, Mike Fitzpatrick, has discovered a fine tool for shaping his attitude toward becoming aware of time and the manner in which it is used. Mike carries a tiny quartz alarm clock on interviews. "It tells my clients I'm time-conscious. They like the novelty of it and the fact that I'm conscious of *their* time as well as my own."

Make it a practice to ask yourself the question, "What should I be doing with my time right now? What is it that *really* needs doing now?" More than anything else, your attitude determines your success in managing time.

Six tools for effective
time management:

- *Goals*
- *Appointment book*
- *Deadlines*
- *Priorities*
- *Secretary*
- *Systems*

Planning Priorities

Planning is decision-making. As Alan Lakein says in his book *How to Get Control of Your Time and Life,* "Control starts with planning. Planning is bringing the future into the present so that you can do something about it now." As a general rule, the more detailed your plan, the better chance that action will follow. Plan your to-do list of priorities for each day the day before. You'll find that it is a good idea to always plan at the same time and same location. Your subconscious mind will respond to this habit pattern and you will find creative planning thoughts beginning to flow. Determine how much time you need for planning each day and put it on your schedule. The "planning hour" will often save several hours of implementing. We recommend using an hour on Friday afternoon for reviewing next week as well as detailing Monday's plan. The purpose of planning is to achieve production, so gear your planning to reach key results.

Staying Effective

The best-kept secret in selling is that unusual success usually follows the individual who determines the few factors that make a significant difference in producing results and who then focuses attention on those key factors most of the time. That's staying effective. There is a difference between efficiency and effectiveness. Efficiency means doing the job right. Effectiveness means doing the *right* job right! *The effective salesperson spends time on the high-payoff activities.*

Your attitude must become one of smoking out the vital tasks and being determined to stay focused on those key factors most of the time. One way of doing this is to make a list of the specific items to be done each day the day before and then decide on the priorities. Sort out those things that must be done. You will discover there is always enough time to do the high-payoff jobs. Ask yourself many times throughout your selling day this key question: "Is this the best use of my selling time right now—am I staying effective?"

Establishing and Maintaining Momentum

You do this best by establishing a daily routine. Decide how to budget your time as you determine hours when you are the most effective. You budget time like you budget money.

Momentum can be safeguarded by finding out what might be wasting your time. Discover your "time leaks." Make a list of "time wasters" you have in a typical day. Study them from the standpoint of how much time they use up. This list will pinpoint activities that need not be done or that could possibly be done by somebody else. Delegate everything possible. It saves time and it develops the roles of others.

Form the habit of avoiding interruptions. Interruptions are momentum stoppers. "The longer I look at time management," said Dr. Kenneth Dunn, Superintendent of Schools in Hewlett, New York, "the more I am impressed with the power of interruptions to kill time."

Remember that your time is valuable. Unnecessary interruptions take a devastating toll. A daily routine that forces productive activity builds momentum.

Developing a Sense of Urgency

Realize the value of deadlines. Imposing deadlines on yourself and experiencing self-discipline in adhering to them aids you in overcoming indecision and procrastination. Give yourself some special reward when a high achievement is reached on time. Stay in a hurry to get things done. Consider these specific "time savers."

- **Become clock-conscious.** Set your watch five minutes fast. It will make you time-conscious and keep you punctual.
- **Don't try to remember everything.** Record appointments and important information.
- **Make every call count.** If you can't make a sale now, determine when you can.
- **Keep your automobile in top condition.** You can't earn commissions if you can't get to your prospect.
- **Become adept at dictating into a pocket cassette recorder.**
- **Make the most of your transition time.** Listen to cassettes during your "in between" time. A remarkable amount of information and inspiration can be obtained during your "scrap time." Turn your automobile into a learning center.
- **Use your secretary as an assistant**—a kind of department head. Besides routine correspondence, phone answering and monitoring of visitors and appointments, a secretary can be invaluable in anticipation and follow-up.
- **Make use of specialists where you lack expertise.** It saves time.
- **Skim books and magazines for ideas.** Learn to skip over unnecessary details and omit copy that's only marginally informative or take a speed reading course. Retain usable ideas and quotations on 3 by 5 index cards.
- **Take advantage of waiting time.** Plan ahead to make this time productive.

- **Generate less paperwork.** Throw away nonessential papers once you have read them.

- **Handle each piece of paper once.** Frequently, a reply to letters can be made on the same sheet of correspondence. Save trivia to be handled on the final day of each month.

- **Avoid "friendly visits."** Many salespeople fall into the trap of looking up friends when they should be making calls.

- **Carry a list of frequently used telephone numbers.** Don't waste time looking up numbers or waiting in line for change.

- **Decide on those responsibilities where you must be accountable and those things that can be delegated.** Then delegate where you can.

- **When you start something, be determined to do it right the first time and do it to a finish.** The old cliché, "If you don't have time to do it right, when will you have time to do it over?" applies today too. Resist the temptation to leave a job unfinished. It takes more time to refamiliarize yourself with a project than to complete it the first time around.

- **Plan unavailability.** Plan a "quiet hour" each day for concentration and creative thinking. It will pay dividends.

Sound principles like those listed above suggest solutions to the time wasters confronting you every day of your selling life.

A MEANINGFUL PARABLE

If you had a bank that credited your account each morning with $86,400, and every evening cancelled whatever amount was still unspent, what would you do? You would draw out every cent every day, of course!

Well, you have such a bank—it's a life bank and it makes a "time deposit" into your account each and every morning. It credits your account with 86,400 seconds. Every night, it rules off as lost any amount you failed to put to a good purpose. It carries no balance forward. It allows no overdrafts.

Each day, it opens a new account for you. Each night, it burns the records of the day. If you fail to use the day's deposit, the loss is yours. There's no going back, no drawing against tomorrow. You must sell in the present on today's deposits. Invest it wisely. Invest it carefully so that you achieve the most return on your investment.

If you'd like to get more value out of your account, reread and restudy this chapter on managing your time. For a quick look at how important your time is, refer to the chart below:

If you earn:	Every hour is worth:	Each minute is worth:	In a year, one hour a day is worth:
$25,000	$12.81	21¢	$3,125
$40,000	$20.49	34¢	$5,000
$50,000	$25.61	43¢	$6,250
$75,000	$38.42	64¢	$9,375
$100,000	$51.23	85¢	$12,500

MANAGING YOUR TIME SUMMED UP

You are paid for what you do—not how many hours you put in. However, of all the hours you spend on your profession, only those actually spent in front of a prospect can make you wealthy. You're able to give yourself a raise (a healthy raise) right now, *if* you can put more selling into the hours you already spend at work.

First, buy or borrow a stopwatch—find out just how little of your time is actually spent in selling. For an entire week, just keep track of your selling time. At the end of the week, reread this chapter—you'll be ready to take remedial action!

Not all of your time is high-quality time. Concentrate your selling into that time—use the low-quality time for routine matters.

Develop a time-consciousness; plan to stay effective, to establish and maintain momentum, to avoid interruptions and to develop a sense of urgency.

When you find out the "routine" or nonproductive things that are costing you time, you will have found the things that are costing you money. You get 86,400 seconds deposited to your account every day—if you don't use them wisely, they're wasted!

MANAGING YOUR TIME REMINDERS

- The quality of selling time is a function of what you spend it doing.
- Develop a time-conscious attitude.
- Plan your priorities daily.
- Stay focused on the essential activities that influence your production.
- Establish and maintain momentum.
- Develop a sense of urgency by setting deadlines.
- A most common time management problem is unnecessary interruptions.

- Make every call count.
- Make the most of your transition time.
- Make use of specialists where you lack expertise.
- Plan a quiet hour each day for creative thinking and self-organization.
- You will discover there is always time to do the high-payoff job.

CHAPTER 11

STAYING UP: KEEP A VITAL SELF-IMAGE AND EXPECT TO WIN

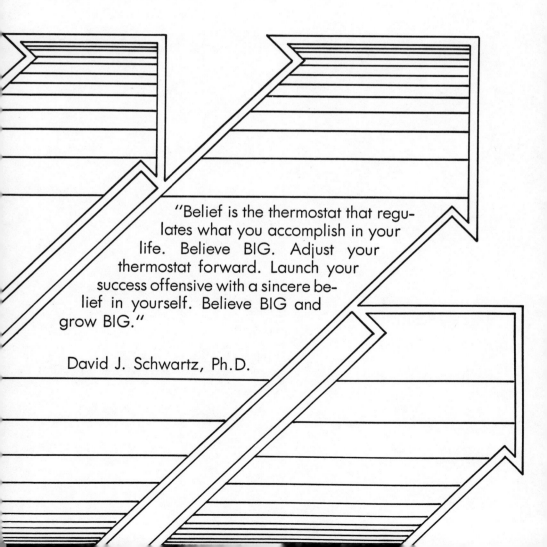

"Belief is the thermostat that regulates what you accomplish in your life. Believe BIG. Adjust your thermostat forward. Launch your success offensive with a sincere belief in yourself. Believe BIG and grow BIG."

David J. Schwartz, Ph.D.

YOUR NEED FOR "UPNESS"

The final gun sounds. The favored team has been upset. Sports writers gather around the dejected coach and ask, "What happened out there today?" The coach struggles for a response and then says, "We were just not up—they were." In the winning dressing room, in answer to the identical question the jubilant reply is, "We were really up—that's the only way to describe it."

The team that finds the way to stay up most of the time is a winner. *Likewise, in selling, upgrading your thinking upgrades your performance, and this produces success.* Your need for "upness" as a professional in selling is just as critical as it is for the professional in any field of endeavor.

We agree with the former all-pro, Bill Glass (now an evangelist and in great demand as a speaker for sales conventions). Bill says, " 'Upness' is a product of self-image and self-motivation. The mind is a most delicate, a most sensitive and amazing mechanism. When your mind works one way it can carry you to outstanding success—when it works another way it can carry you to uninspired performance."

Let's examine ways in which you can build a strong, healthy self-image and stay motivated on a consistent basis.

WHAT IS SELF-IMAGE?

Whether or not you are conscious of it, you carry into every selling situation a rather definite picture of yourself. If asked, you could produce a number of words to describe yourself. It is to be hoped that you think of yourself as an intelligent, informed, competent person. Psychologists agree your self-image is an accurate measure of your personality and your possibilities as a salesperson.

Self-image is how you view yourself. It is how you perceive yourself. Your perception measures the height of your selling possibilities. "A stream cannot rise higher than its source." Nothing else will gear you to accomplish superior selling results as will the belief in your own possibilities. It is here that your selling power originates.

It's important to understand two fundamental principles about self-image:

- **You will be true to your self-image.** You will perform the way you see yourself performing.
- **Your self-image can and does change.**

Since you perform according to your self-image, the key to changing your sales performance lies in changing your self-image.

CHANGING YOUR SELF-IMAGE

Your self-image can be changed by the people with whom you choose to associate. It can be changed by the books you read, cassettes you listen to, TV programs you view. The feedback from all of these things can change your daily performance. Occasionally the change will be dramatic. Most of the time it is gradual—so gradual, in fact, that you may not even notice the change.

A friend of ours underwent a spiritual change in his life five years ago. Some key things changed immediately, others slowly. He told us, "I didn't really realize just how *much* I had changed until I met a man I hadn't seen in about four years. As he began to reminisce about things we had done then, I was mildly shocked. Oh, I had done all of the things he was talking about, but it was so far from my present character that it was as though he were talking about someone else."

The friend paused a moment and added, "I've read that when they make star maps, they first expose a photographic plate, wait a certain length of time and then expose another. Stars move so slowly that it is only by comparing the latest plate with the previous one that you can detect movement. In the same way, my change was so gradual that I wasn't even aware of it."

Dr. Maxwell Maltz, in his best-seller *Psycho-Cybernetics,* talks about the girl who changed her self-image dramatically after plastic surgery on her face. Once her appearance changed, her personality changed. She perceived herself differently. Many people experience change in self-image through religious experiences. Most of the time, however, the changes are gradual. This is why it's important to associate with successful people, read self-improvement books and listen to motivational and inspirational cassettes. As you become more confident, you will gradually perceive yourself as a more effective, persuasive salesperson.

The important motivation you have for changing

your self-image lies in the fact that the great selling results are produced by the perpetual expectation of attaining them. Despite any natural talents, training and education, your selling achievements will never rise higher than your expectations. *The expectant approach, the expectant presentation and the expectant close are what produce the desired results.* People can, who think they can. People can't, who think they can't. This is an unchanging, indisputable law of selling and of life itself.

Through the ages, philosophers have disagreed on many things. But they have had unanimous agreement on one thing: "You become what you think about most of the time." Emerson said, "People become what they think about all day long." In the Bible, we read, "As a man thinketh in his heart, so is he." There's not much question about it—you will perform the way you see yourself performing. You will be true to your self-image.

ONE THING NOT TO SURRENDER

Count as an enemy the person who shakes your expectation of your selling ability. Remember, as a professional salesperson your self-confidence is the one thing you can never afford to surrender. Nothing multiplies a salesperson's ability like faith in himself or herself. It will make a one-talent person into a success—while a ten-talent person without it will fail.

How often have you heard said about some successful person, "Everything he or she touches turns to gold?" We sometimes think of successful people as being lucky. The fact is, their success represents their expectations—it's the sum of their habitual ways of thinking. By the force of their expectations, such persons wring success from the most adverse circumstances.

Expectation brings successful experiences and successful experiences reinforce the power of confidence in selling.

Individuals who are self-reliant, positive, optimistic and assured "magnetize" conditions. They carry in their very presence an air of victory that compounds its power by convincing others. Their poise, assurance and ability increase in direct ratio to the number of selling achievements.

BUILDING YOUR VITAL SELF-IMAGE

There is a seven-step process for building a strong self-image.

1. **Learn to forgive yourself.** It is important not to carry around a guilt complex. Forgive yourself for the little human errors you have made in the past. You have heard that forgiveness is good for the soul. This is certainly true in building a healthy self-image. In this respect, we are not necessarily talking about spiritual forgiveness. We are talking about the forgiveness you give yourself on a daily basis for those little human mistakes that everyone makes from time to time.

Don't dwell on your imperfections. Recognize your good points and be proud of them.

Dr. Leon Teck, the Connecticut psychiatrist, in his book *The Fear of Success* says, "The fear of success can pop up in the most unlikely places." It can be the fear of getting married or being named company president. It can mean fear of winning your weekly tennis game, getting close to a friend, or making an important sale.

The underlying cause, according to Dr. Teck, is that "we were all children once. For a time, we were insignificant. When success finally arrives, we don't quite believe it." Dr. Teck then states the specific reason why most of us don't want to do too well in too many things. He says, "You think you don't deserve it; therefore, you feel guilty about your good fortune. You are afraid of the unearned visibility."

Pamper yourself a little more. You can't be a likable person unless you like yourself. It's almost impossible to like yourself if you cannot discover the way to forgive yourself. The Bible says, "Love thy neighbor as thyself." You can't do a very good job of loving your neighbor if you don't love yourself—can you?

2. **Be able to forgive others.** Don't carry grudges. Remember, you become what you think about. If you carry a grudge, you're likely to become like the person you are carrying the grudge against. The Bible also says, "Forgive us *our* trespasses *as we forgive* those who trespass against *us.*" That's saying, "We know we won't be forgiven if we don't forgive."

A man once said to us, "I hate my former partner but he lives 500 miles away—what possible difference could it make if I forgive him since we never meet?" The difference isn't the difference it might make to him—the difference is the difference it makes to you and your life and attitude.

3. **Develop your ability to communicate.** Express how you feel. We have all experienced the situation when we carry something around inside and all of a

sudden decide to express it. We jump all over someone—maybe someone very close to us. However, when it comes out, we feel better and they feel better. It is important to communicate with others, especially those close to you: your spouse, children and friends. Don't carry feelings inside. Let them come out.

Don't be modest in the way you accept compliments. If someone gives you a compliment, thank the person. Communicate how good he or she made you feel.

It is also important to communicate with yourself. In this regard, ask yourself these questions: "When was the last time I was alone? When was the last time I just sat around and thought about my situation?"

Another area of concern is your spiritual communication. If you pray, communicate with God. We are told that in regard to prayer, there is too much communication from us to God—not enough from God to us. Do a lot of praying and remember to let God do some of the "talking."

4. **Build a life model.** In the next chapter we will recommend writing out your life goals. You'll learn to set realistic goals that you can achieve one step at a time. You'll learn how important it is to have a master dream list. *It is important to put in writing the type of person you want to become as well as the things you want to accomplish.*

5. **Use your imagination in a positive manner.** Become an optimist. When you are down in the dumps, imagine the better times ahead. This will give you the drive to meet challenges. People sometimes say, "I just don't have a good imagination." We ask them, "Do you worry very much?" They reply, "I worry all the time." You see, they *have* a good imagination, they're just using it negatively. *Form the habit of*

using your imagination positively. Visualize yourself accomplishing your goals.

One of the great sales personalities of our time is Mary Crowley. Mary has launched thousands of women into selling careers.

Mary believes in the power of expectation. Mary says, "Expect great things to happen. Boldly predict what you are going to do. Be daring and persistent. You may give out—but never give up!" Then she adds, *"Be determined to be somebody because God never made a nobody."*

6. Compete but don't compare. You should compete with your friends and associates but you should never compare. "Keeping up with the Joneses" adds unneeded pressures to your selling life. Build your life model: *compare your life with what you ought to be.* Many people are frustrated and have nervous breakdowns because they are comparing themselves with other people. Never compare yourself with others—compete with them.

7. Be yourself—but be your best self. It is important to study and learn from other people. It is important to emulate other people, but in the end be yourself. We've heard Dr. Maltz say at our Purdue Institutes, "Be you—because you are the most unique you that God ever made." *Be yourself—but be your best self.*

So, that's the process for building a healthy self-image:

1. Learn to forgive yourself.
2. Be able to forgive others.
3. Develop your ability to communicate.
4. Build a life model.
5. Use your imagination in a positive manner.

6. Compete but don't compare.

7. Be yourself—but be your best self.

Be positive about yourself, your selling job and your future. Be determined to have a strong, healthy self-image.

*"Put forth honest,
intelligent effort."*

BE AWARE OF TWO
MENTAL DISEASES

In building your self-image you must be aware of two obstacles or "mental diseases." One is the disease known as "Mumpsimus." Mumpsimus means "a persistent belief in a mistaken idea." If you go back 500 years, almost everyone had common mumpsimus—they believed the world was flat. Today, some people have a mumpsimus about salespeople: "They're selfish, commission-conscious, aggressive, uneducated, etc." You must be careful not to be affected by this disease. It can be prevented by applying the seven processes for building a healthy self-image that we just discussed.

The second disease is known as "Sniop." Sniop isn't a word, it's an acronym. It describes a person who is *S*usceptible to the *N*egative *I*nfluences of *O*ther *P*eople. We are susceptible to the negative input of other people. One time we were in the office of Hubert Noack, a Sales Training Director in Appleton, Wisconsin. He had a sign on his wall that read: "Don't be SNIOPed by someone who has MUMPSIMUS." This is easy to do. This is why it is important to follow the seven-step formula for building a healthy self-image.

"Don't be SNIOPED by someone who has MUMPSIMUS."

To be an effective salesperson, you must develop a strong, healthy self-image. *See yourself at your best.* Visualize yourself reaching your goals. You were born to win. You deserve to win in selling. You will win by building your self-image.

MOTIVATION COMES FROM WITHIN

Ralph Cordiner, during his reign as Chairman of the Board at General Electric, made a significant statement at a sales conference. "We need from every salesperson a determination to undertake a program of self-improvement. Nobody orders a person to develop. Whether you lag behind or move ahead is a matter of personal choice. Self-development is something which takes time, work and sacrifice. Nobody can do it for you. It calls for self-motivation—the kind of motivation that comes from within."

We have found Mr. Cordiner's advice to be sound. It is practical. Live it. You will reach the top rung of the ladder of production honor rolls by staying motivated. Your company's training programs provide content and method. The acid test is, do they get results? *Results call for execution and execution requires motivation—self-motivation.*

Bobby Knight, the fiery Indiana University basketball coach, thinks the will to win is much overplayed. "What success requires is the will to prepare—to stay motivated." We again add to this: "And all motivation is, in reality, self-motivation."

In a previous book, *First Down, Lifetime to Go,* Roger

said, "You can't just talk positive and be a winner, you have to believe it deep inside." *It's not enough to have the will-to-win—you need the will to work-to-win!*

> **"Spectacular achievements are always preceded by unspectacular preparations."**

SIX STEPS TO SELF-MOTIVATION

Motivation is a desire to achieve, a desire to win, a desire to do well, a desire to perform at your best. The well-known Olympic gold medal winner, our good friend Reverend Bob Richards, talks to athletic coaches all over America. Bob asks each group, "What do you think it takes to make a champion athlete?" Some respond that it's coaching. Others say it's talent. Others say it's natural ability. Others say it's being at the right place at the right time. Bob tells us he is convinced the key ingredient in great athletes is desire. Bob believes that when you find athletes with desire, you have individuals who will take coaching. They will use their talent. They'll make their breaks. They will be self-motivated.

How do you motivate yourself and stay motivated for the long haul? Here is a six-step procedure you can follow:

- **Develop self-acceptance.** The starting point is having respect for yourself. As we discussed earlier, it is vital that you have a strong, healthy self-image. To win in selling, think well of yourself.

- **Realize you have the potential for greatness.** When Roger graduated from Annapolis and entered the Navy for four years of active service, most people thought that the inactivity would signal the end of his career. But Roger never doubted his ability not only to *play* pro football but to play *great* pro football. He said, "I was worried about a lot of things when I reported to my first full training camp in July of 1969. I knew people were saying I couldn't make it back after four years, but I had an unbelievably positive attitude."

- **Plan for greatness.** How do you plan for greatness? By *deciding* to do great things, then doing all of the *small* things that add up to greatness. With Roger, it meant running and doing pushups—more than were required. When Ben Hogan was coming back after an auto accident and doctors didn't expect him to walk again, much less play golf, he painfully practiced hour after hour. He went on to become one of America's all-time great golfers— but he also spent more hours *practicing* than any other golfer!

- **Think like successful people think.** Form the habit of asking yourself: "Is this the way a successful salesperson would do it? What would a successful person do with this idea? How would a successful person deal with this? Am I looking and acting like a person who has maximum self-respect?"

- **Act as if it were impossible to fail.** There are two kinds of confidence—quiet confidence and cocky confidence. Cocky confidence inspires a desire in others to see you *fail*. Quiet confidence inspires others to want to see you *succeed!* Roger, "Mr. Clutch" to his teammates, had a quiet confidence on the field that inspired others to believe that, whatever the circumstances, it was still possible to win.

Roger has taken this same quiet confidence with him into thousands of selling situations. It's not only inspiring, but it's believable. People tend to accept you at *your* assessment of yourself.

- **Monitor your results.** Form the habit of measuring and monitoring your sales results. There is great motivation in taking note of the progress you are making. Studying the score causes the sales score to improve.

"Don't settle for second best."

STAYING UP SUMMED UP

Every salesperson's most important customer is himself or herself. Before you can sell anything to anyone, you must sell yourself on your job, your ability, your product and your future.

We referred in an earlier chapter to Rich DeVos who, along with Jay Van Andel, has built one of the biggest and best sales organizations in the world at Amway. Rich believes respect and enthusiasm are vital characteristics for people involved in selling.

Rich says, "Enthusiasm is relatively more important than product knowledge or experience in sales. I am convinced that to be successful, you must be enthusiastic. If you aren't excited about your job or the products you are selling, you can't expect others to be excited either. Enthusiasm stems from the belief that what you are doing is worthwhile and the products you represent are of high quality and they work. And, enthusiasm is contagious. If a person is committed to his or her goals, others will feel it."

Rich goes on to say, "I believe you achieve that which you think you can achieve. I have learned we must respect each individual with whom we come in contact. It takes all persons from one end of the economic spectrum to the other to make the free enterprise system work. We must have respect for ourselves; respect which will work to generate feelings of self-confidence and create a positive image of our job. Our self-concept is an all-important ingredient in achieving success in selling. The salesperson who respects himself or herself and has faith in his or her responsibility will succeed—be it sales or any other endeavor. Those whose aim is low generally hit their target! Those who expect good things to happen usually make them happen. The ingredients are respect, enthusiastic hard work, a commitment to goals and a strong, healthy self-image."

Bob Coode has been selling life insurance in Cleveland for ten years, and he has qualified for the prestigious Million Dollar Round Table ten times. Bob recently admitted to us that successful salespeople often talk to themselves and "sell themselves" all day long. "We do it to overcome the other negative voices," he said. "Our prospects tell us they don't need our product. They hammer at our confidence and challenge our self-esteem all day long. Smart salespeople talk their confidence up. They remind themselves of the obstacles they first had to conquer to win previous sales. They sell themselves on the answers they'll use for the objections they're certain to face. They build a strong case for imagining a successful conclusion because in their conversation with themselves, they are selling their most suspicious listener."

Bob was saying that a strong, healthy self-image precedes and causes almost all of your selling achievements. You are under the influence of your self-image every minute of your selling day. Everything you see, hear or work with creates an impression that produces a result corresponding to the mental picture you first perceived of yourself.

Your self-image first idealizes what self-motivation afterward realizes. Turn on your imagination. Dial to your most desired scene. Spell out a detailed, vivid action shot of yourself as the motivated salesperson you have always wanted to be. It will prove to be one of the most valuable and productive forms of practice you have ever done.

You'll discover yourself being *up* for every selling situation.

STAYING UP REMINDERS

- Upgrading your thinking upgrades your results.
- "Upness" is a product of self-image and self-motivation.
- Self-image can and does change.
- Learn to forgive yourself and others.
- Build a life model.
- Use your imagination in a positive manner.
- Compete but don't compare.
- Be yourself, but be your *best* self.
- Success requires the will to prepare.
- All motivation is in reality self-motivation.
- Develop self-acceptance as a starting point.
- Realize you have the potential for greatness.
- Monitor your results.
- Keep yourself sold on you.

CHAPTER 12

FIVE STEPS TO PROSPEROUS GOAL SETTING AND ACTION PLANNING

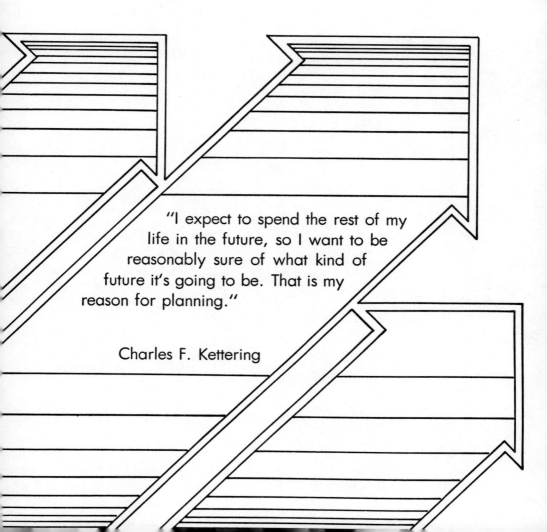

"I expect to spend the rest of my life in the future, so I want to be reasonably sure of what kind of future it's going to be. That is my reason for planning."

Charles F. Kettering

PLAN YOUR FUTURE NOW

The desirable attitude toward your future in selling is summed up in two self-management concepts: goal setting and action planning. When joined together, they form a strong foundation upon which selling success is built.

Experience will teach you that selling success, financial success and happiness are mainly the result of two things:

- persistent effort to develop your personal assets
- setting up and steadfastly pursuing a series of goals for growth

Life doesn't cheat. It doesn't pay in counterfeit coins. It doesn't lock up shop and go home when payday comes. It pays every person exactly what has been earned.

**I bargained with Life for a penny,
And Life would pay no more,
However, I begged at evening
When I counted my scanty store;**

**For Life is a just employer,
He gives you what you ask,**

> **But once you have set the wages,**
>   **Why, you must bear the task.**
>
> **I worked for a menial's hire,**
>   **Only to learn, dismayed,**
> **That any wage I had asked of Life,**
>   **Life would have gladly paid.**
>
> *Jessie B. Rittenhouse*

The old law that you get what you earn hasn't been suspended.

When you take these truths into your business life and believe in them—when you thoughtfully complete the five-step approach to goal setting and action planning developed in this chapter each year—you've turned a big corner on the high road that will lead you straight to success throughout your selling career.

Earl Nightingale reminds us, "Success is the progressive realization of a worthy idea." Goal setting is determining one's worthy ideal. Action planning is the progressive realization of those ideals.

Goal setting and action planning are as inseparable as night following day, yet equally distinctive. They are the head and tail of the same coin. One says "what" and the other says "how." Together, they say "success."

An individual without goals is like a ship without a captain. The ship may well have the finest equipment and design, yet without a captain to steer and chart its course to a designated port, it goes nowhere—and may even drift aimlessly onto the shoals.

Goal setting establishes your chief aims. It determines your purposes—your worthy ideals. Without such aim, your life will be like an abandoned ship at sea, tossed by the waves of circumstance, often taking the voyage of least resistance.

The key is direction and focus. An individual with growth goals is an individual with determination and drive. Goals for growth animate and invigorate. Your effectiveness and productivity are greatly multiplied when you have singleness of purpose. Tunnel vision is good when your target is clearly sighted.

Goal setting is the initial cause of which success is the final effect.

HOW YOU SET GOALS

Now that you have an understanding of the importance of goal setting, what are some of the criteria to appraise in establishing your chief aims? There are four factors, equally important, in goal setting.

1. Your Goals Must Be Achievable

Why push and strive toward a goal if you know that it is outside of your reach? Properly established goals are attainable only with a maximum effort. They push you to give your optimal level of effort. They have been set realistically high. Vince Lombardi stated, "I firmly believe that any man's finest hour, his greatest fulfillment to all he holds dear, is the moment when he has worked his heart out in a good cause and lies exhausted on the field of battle victorious."

Your goals must push you to your maximum, yet reward you with the satisfying taste of victory when you grasp them—but they *must be attainable*.

As Roger says, "If you're the bottom salesperson on the ladder, a reasonable goal isn't to be the top producer in an office of 100 salespeople in a year. Maybe your first goal should be to make the top twenty— then the top ten.

"If you're a football team and your record is 4 and 8, your goal can't be to make the Superbowl that year—a reasonable goal might be to be 8 and 8.

"The Cowboys always have high goals, but they are attainable. We won a Superbowl one year when we were 4 and 3—it was a long way to go but it was attainable and we knew it. We didn't just have an overall goal—we have goals for each player—they're high goals, measurable goals and yet achievable goals."

2. Your Goals Must Be Believable

"We went into the locker room of a team one year when we were playing in the Superbowl and they had goals right in the locker room—but they were unreasonable. They hadn't been a very strong team the year before but they had exceptionally high goals for the next year that were just unbelievable. Their goals were, in many areas, tougher than ours, and we were a championship team!

"A goal that's not believable will have a negative impact on you."

This is closely related to the first criterion. A goal should reflect realism, not idealism. It must be something you are *convinced* you can reach.

3. Your Goals Must Be Measurable

Think about your favorite athletic event. Would you find it interesting if there were no scoreboard? What makes the game exciting is knowing the score and how much time is remaining. Your goals will become challenging only when they are measurable.

4. Your Goals Must Have Deadlines

Time is your most precious commodity. It can never be replaced. If you are to use your time most productively, your goals must have deadlines. Deadlines bring compulsion and a responsible commitment of action.

"Build a program of self-development."

THE FIVE KEY STEPS TO GOAL SETTING AND ACTION PLANNING

Again, for the sake of emphasis, remember that there are two chief cornerstones that support success. Goal setting sharpens your focus—your plan of action gets you there. In this chapter we will cause you to first evaluate yourself and determine what your life dreams actually are. Next, you will establish a plan of action to achieve your goals. Finally, you will determine the effort required in weekly compartments to achieve these goals.

This must become an annual planning discipline. It is serious business. It requires careful thought. So, begin now—plan the balance of this year and your future now!

Step One: Looking at Me

The first priority on your road to selling success is to realistically evaluate yourslf. There is no substitute for your being completely introduced to your greatest asset: *you!*

Before you can determine where you want to go and

how and when you want to get there, you must first know from where you're starting. The captain of a ship can't chart a course for a distant land without first knowing exactly *where* he or she is *now*. You can't chart a course for the future without knowing where you are, either.

You find where you are by taking personal inventory.

Catalog your needs, interests, strengths and weaknesses. Once you have done this, you can develop ways to meet your needs, satisfy your interests, build on your strengths and strengthen your weaknesses. You're ready to chart your course!

On the pages that follow, we'll conduct a self-analysis in three key areas: business, personal and financial. This exercise will serve as a mirror with which to view yourself.

> *"The picture is never greater than the artist. You improve the work by first improving the worker."*

BUSINESS SELF-ANALYSIS

This proficiency checklist is to serve as a self-inventory of your skills and abilities. Its purpose is to determine the performance/potential gap in your selling. Rate yourself on a scale from 1 to 5 for the following items and then compare your score with the perfect score of 100.

1. Displaying a commanding professional presence   1 2 3 4 5
2. Setting reachable goals with established deadlines   1 2 3 4 5
3. Planning my work the previous day   1 2 3 4 5
4. Prospecting effectiveness   1 2 3 4 5
5. Pre-approach efficiency   1 2 3 4 5
6. Skill in probing for facts   1 2 3 4 5
7. Handling the preparation process   1 2 3 4 5
8. Sales presentation effectiveness   1 2 3 4 5
9. Meeting objections   1 2 3 4 5
10. Closing skill   1 2 3 4 5
11. Obtaining referrals   1 2 3 4 5
12. Use of weekly activity and result report to determine "dollar value" of each selling activity and progress made toward goals   1 2 3 4 5
13. Efficient office administration   1 2 3 4 5
14. Secretarial, telephone, mail services   1 2 3 4 5
15. Letter writing   1 2 3 4 5
16. Staying active in business, civic and church activities   1 2 3 4 5
17. Reading, study and cassettes   1 2 3 4 5
18. Physical fitness program   1 2 3 4 5
19. Managing personal financial affairs   1 2 3 4 5
20. Personal planned self-improvement program   1 2 3 4 5

TOTAL POSSIBLE SCORE   100

MY SCORE   _____

Performance/Potential Gap   _____

PERSONAL SELF-ANALYSIS

Personal Statistics: Age ____ Height ____ Weight ____

Personal Priority Ranking:

____ career   ____ family   ____ spiritual

____ social   ____ physical   ____ knowledge

Greatest personal motivation and interests:

_____

_____

Personal strengths:

_____

_____

Personal responsibilities:

_____

_____

Personal accomplishments of which I am most proud:

_____

_____

Areas that I must strengthen:

_____

_____

Personal projects, activities, or hobbies that I plan to initiate:

_____

_____

Personal habits that I plan to build into my life:

_____

_____

Planned personal accomplishments for/with my family:

_____

_____

FINANCIAL SELF-ANALYSIS

(It is essential that you know your family financial position. The NET WORTH of YOU, INC., is the difference between what you own and what you owe.)

ASSETS (what you own)
Cash:
    Checking Accounts .... $_____
    Savings Accounts .... _____
U.S. Government Bonds (accrued
    value) .... _____
Stocks (market value) .... _____
Bonds (market value) .... _____
Life Insurance (cash value) .... _____
Real Estate—Home (market value) .. _____
Other Real Estate (market value) .... _____
Automobiles (market value) .... _____
Personal Property (furniture, jewelry,
    appliances, furs, etc.) .... _____
Amounts Owed You .... _____
Other: _____ .... _____

Total Assets .... $_____

LIABILITIES (what you owe)
Current Bills (amount owed) .... $_____
Installment Debt (balance owed)
    Automobile .... _____
    Home Improvement .... _____
    Personal .... _____
    Furniture, Appliance .... _____
    Other: _____ .... _____
Mortgage (balance owed) .... _____
Other Real Estate (balance owed) ... _____
Other Amounts Owed: _____ _____

Total Liabilities .... $_____

TOTAL ASSETS .... $_____

TOTAL LIABILITIES .... − $_____

NET WORTH .... = $_____

Step Two: Examining Your Dreams

Your full potential often lies dormant until aroused by your dreams. In the initial step, you took a look forward to the person you can become. You'll see even more.

Remember, "Success is the progressive realization of a worthy ideal." Focus your attention now on what you believe to be life's worthy ideals for you.

In order to do so, allow your mind the freedom of dreaming. What are your life's dreams? What do you have visions of achieving? Lewis Carroll said, "It's a poor sort of memory that only works backwards." *Project yourself mentally into the future.* What would you like to see accomplished in your life?

It is important for a person to dream of what they want to do because, as Homer Rice, the Georgia Tech Athletic Director, says, "People are motivated to do what they themselves decide to do."

On the following pages, you will compile your "Master Dream List." Remember, your only limitations are self-imposed. It is important that you consider everything you will want to do—everything you will want to learn—everything you will want to earn—yes, and everything you will want to become.

You make your dreams—and then your dreams make you.

Dreams are like stars for the seafaring mariner on a dark night. You will use them for direction to safely reach your destination.

Precise yet perceptive is the proverb that states, "Without a vision, the people perish."

BUILDING YOUR MASTER DREAM LIST*

I want to own: _____

_____

_____

I want to know: _____

_____

_____

I want to do: _____

_____

_____

I want to be: _____

_____

_____

I want to earn: _____

_____

_____

I want to learn: _____

_____

_____

*Compliments of Homer Rice, Vice President and Director of Athletics at Georgia Tech.

Step Three: Establishing This Year's Goals

Next, you clarify your objectives. Having established life's chief aims, you must realign your thinking to the present—to this year. *The future is where you dream. Now, this year, is where you live and where you must perform.*

Yearly goals bridge the gap between where you are now and where you want to go in life. They put you on schedule to achieve your life's objectives. Few people know what they want. Still fewer know when they want it.

A financial budget is a key in determining your yearly goals. Before you can set intelligent sales goals, you must first know what your financial needs are. A yearly budget will show you what you must produce, as a *minimum.*

Remember, a controlled inflow, regardless of how great, with an uncontrolled outflow leaves any river dry.

As you establish your personal goals for this year, you will always find it helpful to establish two kinds of goals—minimum and superior.

Your minimum goals are what you must do this year. It is what you will do regardless. *Your minimum goals are committed goals.* They are set realistically high and require a complete dedication to their achievement. There is no room for compromising your minimum goals.

On the other hand, your superior goals are flavored with optimism. These are the things that you would hope to achieve, those things over and above your minimum goals. *Superior goals are bonus goals.*

You will want to give careful thought to your minimum and superior goals. They are small keys that will unlock big futures in selling.

My Budget for This Year (Minimum Income Requirements)	Monthly Average	Annual
Mortgage Payments or Rent		
Household Expenses & Maintenance		
Utilities, Including Fuel		
Food		
Clothing		
Children's School-Related Expenses		
Personal Care, Cleaning, etc. .		
Education, Reading, Dues & Subscriptions		
Entertainment & Recreation, Vacation		
Personal Expenses (Lunch, etc.)		
Auto, Transportation		
Gifts & Contributions		
Medical & Dental, Health Insurance		
Personal Life Insurance, Savings, Investment		
Debt Reduction, Loan Payments		
Taxes		
Business Expenses (Not Reimbursed)		
Miscellaneous		

TOTAL INCOME NEEDED THIS YEAR $_____

My Superior Goal $_____

THIS YEAR'S SPECIFIC GOALS

KEY SELLING GOALS*	MINIMUM	SUPERIOR
New Calls	_____	_____
New Customers	_____	_____
Unit Sales	_____	_____
Service Calls	_____	_____
Commission Earnings	$_____	$_____
Bonus Earnings	$_____	$_____
Other Income	$_____	$_____
Total Income	$_____	$_____

SELF-DEVELOPMENT GOALS*

The selling skills I will develop this year will include the following:

_____

_____

The knowledge I will acquire this year will be in these areas:

_____

_____

The habits I will strengthen include the following:

_____

_____

The most effective way for me to reach and surpass each of the above goals is:

_____

_____

*Can be further personalized to your particular field.

236

"Our business in life is to get ahead of ourselves—to break our own records, to outstrip our yesterday by our today, to do the little parts of our work with more force than ever before."

Step Four: Fixing the Action Plan

Briefly, retrace your steps. You have taken an inventory of where you are presently. You have looked at your dreams and seen where you would like to go. You have determined what you must do this year to advance toward achieving your goals.

Now, you take the process one step further. You move one step closer to success. *"What is it that I must do each week in order to accomplish my goals for this year?"*

You have planned your work. Now you must work your plan. When you meet goals on a weekly basis, your year becomes successful. *It is here—with each week's activity and results—that the battle is won.*

Therefore, you must fix a weekly plan of action that will ensure your success. A Weekly Effort Formula becomes indispensable. Obviously, no pat formula can be developed that will be adaptable to every person who enters the field of selling. The activity requirement necessary for success varies according to the nature of your business, your previous experience, your background and your markets. Then, too, this requirement changes as you gain experience, knowledge, skills and confidence.

However, it does serve your best interest if your activity can be measured against a clearly defined standard. A Weekly Effort Formula, when calculated, can be a very helpful self-management tool.

In Frederickton, Canada, George Haynes told us about how much he hates the telephone. "I despise it—but my weekly calculations tell me that I make $45.20 every time I pick it up. This weekly reminder is the only motivation I need to pick up the telephone many times every day."

On the next page, we show you how to set up and live by a Weekly Effort Formula that will show you where your profits lie.

As you look at your Weekly Effort Formula, you will see that it pays to play the odds. The more contacts you make, the more opening interviews you'll get— and the more opening interviews you have, the more closing interviews you'll have. The more closing interviews you have, the more sales you'll make— and the more sales you make, the more commissions you'll earn!

A former associate of ours and a multimillion-dollar producer in Detroit, Bill Mansfield, claims, "The most important factor in selling success is *a firm belief in the law of averages.*" Bill goes on to say, "Top salespeople know that if they are prepared, a certain number of calls will inevitably result in a certain number of interviews—leading to a certain number of sales."

Roger tells how he became a percentage player in football. It was the 1970 season and Los Angeles beat Dallas just as they broke camp. Roger played in the second period and threw a long touchdown pass to Margene Adkins. Later, just as the half was ending, Roger threw an interception.

"Why did you throw the ball?" Coach Landry asked him as he came off the field.

"Wait a second, Coach," Roger said, "I wanted to go for the touchdown."

DEFINITIONS

Pre-approach—a call to arrange an appointment.

Opening interview—a probing, fact-finding interview to determine whether or not you have a prospect. A prospect is one who recognizes a need, has the ability to make a decision, and is salable by you.

Closing interview—the presentation of your recommendation and closing of the sale.

WEEKLY EFFORT FORMULA

Personal Observation
Direct Mail
Referred Leads

Friends & Aquaintances
Client Leads
Cold Canvass

STANDARDS
FOR MY FIELD

MY
FORMULA

Contacts

Opening
Interviews

Closing
Interviews

Sales

Commission
Earnings $_____

HONEST, INTELLIGENT EFFORT IS ALWAYS REWARDED.

"That's not the percentage thing to do," Landry said. "The percentage thing to do is run out the clock and wait for another chance in the second half. Now you've given them the ball and they can score by kicking a field goal."

Learn to play the percentages—go after the big ones, the ones where your chances of making it are good.

The Jones Game Plan of Action

George Jones of Des Moines shared his strategy for setting goals with us.

George reached for his billfold, pulled out a card and told us about his idea. "I review this card daily and revise it quarterly. The card is divided into three sections—my life goals, my goals for this year and the game plan of action that must be taken now in order to reach these goals."

George takes an hour each month to reason the priority goals. "This system has been responsible for me making the Million Dollar Round Table, enjoying better health and staying goal-directed."

This is a simple but powerful idea that has propelled George Jones to a position of leadership in his company. It will do the same for you.

Here is the card George Jones took from his billfold:

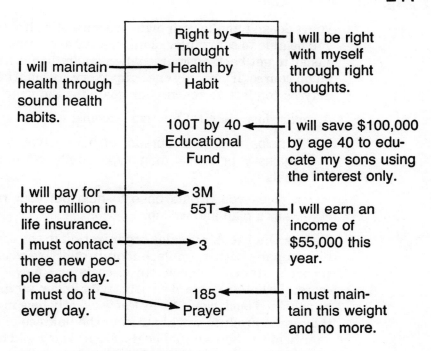

Step Five: Keeping Records to Break Records

You have laid the two chief cornerstones—goal setting and action planning—upon which you will build a successful year. There are no secrets to this kind of strategy—absolutely none. Honest, intelligent effort is always rewarded in selling. It is the law of laws: the law of cause and effect.

It now becomes a matter of (1) staying focused on the priority tasks and (2) measuring your results weekly, because measurement always improves performance.

You need a system of checkups to stay informed of your progress. Just as the stadium scoreboard tells the athlete the score and how much time is left, so will a system of weekly checkups gauge your progress.

Many companies furnish salespeople with a report form for recording weekly activities and results. If yours doesn't, make your own—because it's vital that you be able to constantly monitor your activities. It's easier to get back on course when you're just a little bit off course. If you only check up every six months, it may be too late to reach your goals for the year!

A report form is vital for two reasons:

- It helps you keep abreast of how you're doing against your weekly, monthly, quarterly and annual goals.

- It gives you a data base to help put your next week's plan into writing.

Tyrone Olier took his sales organization to the top of his company with a simple, but quite effective weekly report system. "Each of our associates knows the score, the dollar value of each activity and what must be achieved each week. They know exactly how much they must produce weekly during the balance of the year to meet their annual goals. Each is now sold that *measurement* improves *performance*."

Like an Olympic athlete who trains for years to win the gold medal and break records, you too must discipline and challenge yourself to pursue your purpose. Records are broken by those who are compelled and driven by their purpose in life. This is your "ownership benefit" in keeping weekly records of your progress. Keeping important records produces consistency—and consistency always produces satisfying results.

GOAL SETTING AND ACTION PLANNING SUMMED UP

"I find the great thing in this world is not so much where you stand as in what direction you are moving. To

**reach the port of heaven, we must sail
sometimes with the wind and sometimes against it—but we must sail—
and not drift, nor lie at anchor."**

Oliver Wendell Holmes said that, and it's never been truer than in the field of selling. Heading in the right direction in your sales career requires only that you fix your eyes upon your goal, visualize it with every ounce of your being, and set out toward its achievement.

Become a kind of sponge for information and ideas that will help you on your way. You don't have to waste years in making mistakes in selling that others have made before you. You will be surprised at how quickly you can reach and surpass your goals. But don't be impatient. Know and have faith that what should come to you will come to you in time. Everything in business works on the side of the salesperson who works with nature's laws.

Above all—if you should forget everything else— remember that everything about you, everything you will ever own, know or experience, operates as a result of the law of cause and effect. As Emerson wrote, "Let each learn a prudence of high strain. Let each learn that everything in nature, even dust and feathers, goes by law and never by luck . . . and that what a person sows, he reaps."

That's it—that's all there is to it. Take stock of your present situation, for it is nothing more or less than the result of your past sowing. Then, you decide what you must sow—today and tomorrow and the next day—and in the sowing you know with certainty that having sown you will then reap the rich results . . . the abundant harvest *must* come.

GOAL SETTING AND
ACTION PLANNING REMINDERS

- Success can best be defined as the progressive realization of a worthy ideal.
- Goals should be set realistically high. They must be believable.
- The first step in clarifying life goals involves self-analysis.
- Your full potential often lies dormant until aroused by building your master dream list.
- Before you can set intelligent sales goals, you must first establish your financial needs.
- Minimum goals are always committed goals.
- Superior goals are bonus goals.
- A Weekly Effort Formula is essential.
- Discipline yourself to calculate the activity and production results you must make happen each week for the balance of the year to reach your important goals.
- The great thing in selling is not where you stand, but the direction in which you are headed.

CHAPTER 13

THE THIRTEEN WINNING TRAITS OF SUPER SALESPEOPLE

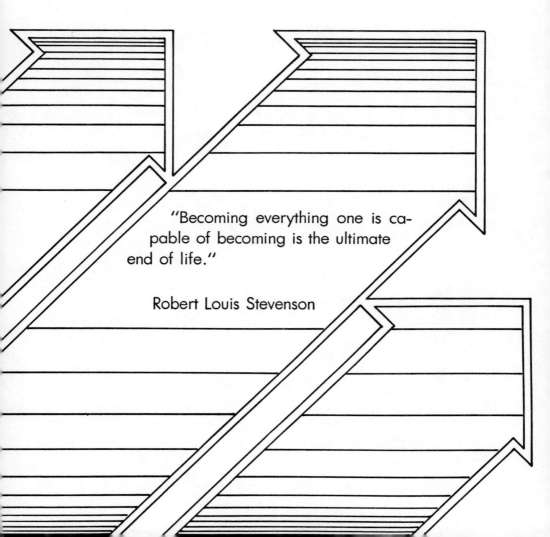

"Becoming everything one is capable of becoming is the ultimate end of life."

Robert Louis Stevenson

WHAT I'VE GOT: WHAT IT TAKES

In the opening chapter, we indicated that many people have a mistaken idea that star performers in selling are born, not made. No doubt you have had an "off day" or two which caused you to have serious doubts about whether you really "measured up" to the role of "super salesperson." Of course, your mythical star salesperson:

- has a magical sales personality
- has a sure-fire sales strategy
- is a mental giant
- is never discouraged
- never fails
- always makes the sale

No real-life individual in sales, no matter how good, can possibly measure up to such a distorted, unrealistic profile.

Every individual in our selling profession carries around a very definite mental picture of "what I've got" and "what it takes" as it relates to being a successful salesperson. Dr. Maxwell Maltz, the recognized authority on self-image psychology, talked to us about this. Dr. Maltz said, "Look around and take a really objective view of the stars in selling. Quickly, you will conclude that they are not really super human. The qualities necessary for success in selling can be developed by anyone. Don't fall into the trap of measuring yourself against a myth!"

"Self-confidence is high on the list of necessary skills," says David Mitchell, Chairman of the Board and Chief Executive Officer for Avon Products, Inc. Mr. Mitchell goes ahead to point out, "This is often an acquired or developed asset. It is gained through experience, and *is constantly reinforced and challenged by both success and failure.* Yes, failure. For the high achiever, disappointment can become a self-induced incentive stimulating the person to reevaluate former concepts and strive toward accomplishing the next goal."

THIRTEEN WINNING TRAITS

Our years of experience have taught us that winners in selling have 13 characteristics in common. As you examine each one, you'll discover that they're traits anyone can develop. It makes no difference how much education or experience you have, or what you have accomplished in your career up to this point. You too can develop and possess these traits.

The 13 winning traits of super salespeople are:

1. **Be and stay committed to goals.**
   Know what you want to achieve. Be totally committed to that goal. View defeat as a temporary thing. It's not so much where you stand, but rather the direction in which you are headed. It's stretching that develops your potential, and it's a complete commitment to realistically high goals that will

cause you to stretch. Measure the progress you are making toward the achievement of your goals. Do this regularly. *Measurement always improves performance.*

2. Be and stay self-disciplined.
Self-discipline is developed when you stop doing what you know you should not do, and start doing what you know you should—whether you like it or not. The degree of your success in selling depends on your ability to recognize those few primary activities that make the big difference in producing results. Self-discipline causes you to concentrate on these activities. *It is forming the habit of doing the right things right.* It is having always a sense of urgency.

3. Be and stay knowledgeable.
Spectacular results in selling are always preceded by unspectacular preparation. Continually accumulate usable information. It gives you a competitive edge. Have the facts and figures ready before plunging into an interview. *Never let a day pass without having learned something new about your product line or services.* Do your homework. Question people who know. People respect the person who is well informed. Be the best-informed salesperson your prospects ever meet. You'll earn their respect and gain their business.

4. Be and stay a relationship-builder.
Build the trust level in all you do. Prospects buy from the individual they trust. Earn the reputation of being 100 percent reliable. *Your success in selling calls for you to be an initiator, an activator, an influencer of attitudes and behaviors.* You function in these roles best by being an effective relationship-builder.

5. **Be and stay self-confident.**
Do this by feeding your mind regularly just as you feed your body. This enables you to accept rejection without too much inner anguish. Use your imagination positively. Remind yourself that you are prepared, poised and persuasive. Your biggest asset is a positive, courageous attitude. This, more than anything else, determines your success in selling. Shakespeare wrote, "Our doubts are traitors, and make us lose the good we oft might win, by fearing to attempt." Confidence is not the absence of fear, it is the conquest of fear. Do the thing you're afraid of and you'll develop the confident, winning feeling.

6. **Be and stay enthusiastic.**
Generate an excitement about what you are selling. It will overcome many shortcomings. Enthusiasm will encourage others to cooperate with you. *Act the way you want to feel.* To be enthusiastic— act enthusiastically.

7. **Be and stay an assistant buyer.**
Prospects are best convinced by reasons they themselves discover. Build the trust level as quickly as possible. Then assist the buyer in recognizing a need and acting upon the solution. Prospects are interested in discussing their business with you only when you indicate by your questions that you intend to show how your proposition will benefit them. *Your aim is always client-building. Customer satisfaction is your stock-in-trade.*

8. **Be and stay perceptive.**
Form the habit of paying attention. Let your "mental radar" work full time. *Deliberately train your eyes to see and your ears to hear.* Develop an

exhaustive observation. It will earn you great dividends.

9. **Be and stay a skillful communicator.**
   You sell with words and expressions. Study both carefully. *You must gain the prospect's understanding and understanding depends on what you say and how you say it.* Express your ideas and recommendations in terms of the self-interest of your prospects. This will cause them to think and act favorably toward you.

10. **Be and stay a perfectionist.**
    Demand excellence of yourself. It attracts and builds credibility. *Don't tolerate mediocrity.* There's no room for compromise among professionals. Stamp your work with excellence.

11. **Be and stay physically fit.**
    Develop the capacity to work hard and long. *Be a self-starter who displays a high continuing level of drive.* As Lombardi said, "Fatigue makes cowards of us all." Diet. Exercise. Run.

12. **Be and stay financially sound.**
    Personal budget-keeping is back in style. It is increasingly essential for you to get the maximum benefit from your selling income and to protect your savings. Do not rely strictly on the instinctive sense of money management. *Get a good handle on your living and business expenses along with your anticipated earnings.* Develop a plan of control over your spending. You will then make progress toward the kind of living which means the most to you.

13. **Be and stay persistent.**
    Always bounce back. In selling, failure means very little if success comes eventually. Resolve to perform what you should; perform without fail that

which you resolve. *Get up when you fall down.* If you get into the game—*stay in!* The secret of success is constancy of purpose.

Back to the strategy that assures victory for you!

The Autobiography of Benjamin Franklin tells us Franklin thought of himself as a very simple man of only ordinary talent. However, like all great individuals, he believed he could achieve success only if he could come upon a strategy that would compel him to obey the essential principles of successful living. Having an imaginative mind, Benjamin Franklin devised a simple but practical strategy that anyone can use. He chose *13* subjects that he felt were important to develop and master. He focused for a week on each subject, which enabled him to go through his entire list four times a year. (Just as we did with our 13 winning traits!) In his final days, Franklin wrote, "This strategy is scientifically sound. Adopt it and you will have taken a sure step toward greatness."

Goethe said, "Before you do something great, you must become something great." Franklin's "focus strategy" moves you toward becoming someone great. *This strategy develops inner motivation. It is this inner motivation that literally moves you toward success!*

IMPROVING YOUR FIELD POSITION

The U.S. Constitution says that we believe that "all men are created equal"—and so they are. But all men and women do not *remain* equal. We firmly believe that, regardless of your "field position" in life now, you can win from where you stand, *if* you begin putting into practice the principles we've been discussing in this book.

We've not put together merely ideas, but workable ideas, ideas that have worked for the three of us, ideas that have worked for thousands of others.

Roger has always said, "Field position of life is important. In football it's great to have ideal field position. As a quarterback it enhanced my chances of moving our team to a touchdown. After the 1972 Superbowl, I kidded Chuck Howley about how he intercepted Bob Griese's pass and made a long run down the sideline, only to fall a little short of the goal line. I told him, 'You could have scored, but you just wanted to give the offense good field position. You wanted your old roommate to be the hero.'

"Well, when God puts us on this earth, he gives some of us good field position and others he doesn't. It's tougher for those who don't have it, but if they still try to do something with their lives, God will reward them some day."

When you look back at Raul Jimenez with a seventh-grade education, trying to make a go of a business in a world full of educated people, you realize that he didn't have very good field position for scoring—yet he now heads a multimillion-dollar-a-year business.

When you look back at W. W. Clements, Chairman of the Board of the Dr Pepper Company, driving a delivery truck in Tuscaloosa, Alabama, you might think he didn't have very good field position—but look at how he scored!

When you look at Carl Joseph, the one-legged football player from Madison High, you might think that he had pretty poor field position—yet he became a football, basketball and track star!

Look at Roger, coming back from the Navy or from surgery—or Tommy John, whose arm was hanging literally by a thread—pretty poor field position, wasn't it? But they went on to win!

Do *you* think *you* have poor field position? You can overcome it from whatever your background, whatever your market, whatever your experience, whatever your past record—*if you want to badly enough!*

You can make it in spite of poor field position—*if* you have made up your mind to succeed.

We want to tell you the greatest sports story of all time.

Charley Paddock had a dream as a little boy. He said, "I want to be a gold medal winner at the Olympics." He went to his coach. "What can I do to be a gold medal winner?" Charley Paddock made the necessary sacrifices. He worked on getting his knees up. He worked on his start. To make the story short, Charley Paddock won the gold medal.

Now listen to it from this point on.

Paddock went around the country saying, "If you've got a dream, if you think you can do something—you can!" A boy in Cleveland, Ohio, came out of the audience and said, "I want to be an Olympic champion too!" Charley Paddock touched the young boy on the shoulder and said, "You can if you'll work, if you'll dream." The young boy was Jesse Owens, who won *four* Olympic gold medals in Germany!

Jesse came back home to Cleveland. Driving down the street in a ticker-tape parade, up came a nine-year-old boy. He put his hands on the side of the car and said, "Gee, Mr. Owens, I would give anything if I could be a champion like you!" Jesse touched this boy's hand and said, "You can if you will work. If you think you can, you can." It was Harrison Dillard who broke Jesse Owens' Olympic record in 1948 and who won another gold medal in 1952.

Harrison Dillard was giving speeches about faith and dreaming and how important it is to life. In Gary, Indiana, the son of a Methodist minister walked up to him and said, "Gee, Mr. Dillard, I would give anything if I could be a champion like you!" It was Lee Calhoun. Lee won the Olympics, breaking Harrison Dillard's record in 1956 and 1960.

Hayes Jones saw a picture of Lee Calhoun. He put it on the wall and said, "I want to be like Lee Calhoun!" He wrote him a letter and Lee wrote him back. He said, "If you will have faith and think that you can, you can." Hayes Jones became an Olympic champion.

Seven Olympic games where one man told another he could—and he did! Where one man had faith and he touched somebody else—they in turn had faith. They are all in the Hall of Fame now. They should call it the "Hall of Inspiration" or the "Hall of Positive Thinking" because that is where it's at. It's the way you think that makes the big difference in sports, in selling and in life.

Here is an unbelievable story. Yet it is so typical of the psychology of a champion and the power of the made-up mind. Bruce Jenner was in Graceland College, Iowa—a little school hardly anyone knew— pretty poor field position. He went down to the Kansas Relays and saw an athlete with a blue USA uniform on. He said, "Boy, I want to become a member of the Olympic team! I want to wear that uniform!" Don't laugh, many of the great performers in history were inspired by the sight of an Olympic uniform. Bruce worked and he made the team. He went to Munich and finished tenth.

While he was there, the magic of the mind began to work. He saw the other athletes. He said, "I can run as fast as they can! I'm as strong as they are! If I put my mind to it and my body in it, I can break the world's record. I can win a gold medal!"

Bruce Jenner came home and wrote down on a piece of paper what he had to do in ten events if he was going to shatter the world record in the decathlon in Montreal four years later.

> 10.6 in the 100 meter
> 23'7" long jump
> 6'7½" high jump
> 49.5 quarter
> 52' shot put
> 162 discus
> 14.5 hurdles
> 15'7" pole vault
> 215 javelin
> 4:16 in the 1500 meter

That's what he wrote down on a piece of paper—and that's what he programmed in his mind.

In Eugene, Oregon, in 1975, he hit every mark within a quarter of an inch or a tenth of a second and broke the world's record.

Then he said, "I've got to better myself in six events if I'm going to beat Aveloff of Russia—if I'm going to win the Olympics." Well, he missed—he only bettered himself in five events—he missed the sixth one by a *whole half inch!*

Now here is our question. Would he have accomplished all of this if he had not mentally programmed himself specifically to an exact time and an exact height? Or was the power of the mind the most important thing in that performance—even more important than his field position in Graceland, Iowa?

The answer is rather obvious.

Mary Kay Ash, founder of Mary Kay Cosmetics and the leader of one of the most dynamic sales organizations in America today, talked to us about this matter of attitude. Mary Kay said, "I believe most people never even begin to tap their full potential because of their lack of faith in their own abilities. God placed within us tremendous ability—and unfortunately most of us die with music still unplayed. It is said that only 10 percent of the potential we have is ever really tapped. As a potential salesperson or possibly someone already in the sales field, the first thing is to believe in yourself and your product. After that, you can and you will convey the same belief to your prospects and customers."

THE MOST MOTIVATIONAL

Every field of human endeavor is led by a relatively small percentage of the people in it. The sales field is no exception. Historically, it has divided itself into two groups: (1) those who lead rich, rewarding and interesting lives and (2) those who live average and largely unrewarding lives.

One time we were talking about these two groups with Bob Richards, the former Olympic champion. The discussion centered on this question: "What is the strongest motivational thought a salesperson can carry with himself or herself?" Think about it for a minute. You are determined to join the top group of salespeople who know more, do more and have more. A successful career is made up of successful days. Now, again, **"What is the strongest motivational thought a salesperson can carry with himself or herself?"**

Well, we discussed this at some length. Here are a few of the thoughts that surfaced near the top of our list:

- Honest, intelligent effort is always rewarded.
- It's not where you stand, it's the direction in which you are headed.
- If you can get in the game—stay in.
- You can alter your performance by altering your mental attitude.
- Get up when you fall down.
- When it's dark enough, you can see the stars.

Finally, we reached unanimous agreement. We concluded that the strongest motivational thought of all was this one:

GOD IS WITH ME

Carry this thought with you and watch the change it will make in your life. You were born to win. God is with you and wants you to have an abundant life.

This leads to our wish for you. It's the same for you as it is for our associates, our families and ourselves. Our wish is that the God who programmed you to win—the God who computerized you to succeed—the God who made it possible for you to conquer death itself—that God will be with you this day and every day throughout your selling career.

All the best to you always!

INDEX